SUPER-DUTY EARTHMOVERS

ERIC C. ORLEMANN

MBI Publishing Company

GC DJ HJ TH JH *illegible* JP JL

First published in 1999 by MBI Publishing
Company, 729 Prospect Avenue, PO Box 1,
Osceola, WI 54020-0001 USA

MBI Publishing Company books are also available
at discounts in bulk quantity for industrial or sales-
promotional use. For details write to Special Sales
Manager at Motorbooks International Wholesalers
& Distributors, 729 Prospect Avenue, Osceola, WI
54020-0001 USA.

Library of Congress Cataloging-in-Publication Data

Orlemann, Eric C.
        Super-duty earthmovers / Eric C. Orlemann.
            p.   cm.
        Includes index.
        ISBN 0-7603-0645-1 (alk. paper)
        1. Earthmoving machinery. 2. Excavating
machinery. 3. Mining machinery. I. Title.
        TA725.0695   1999
        621.1'52'028—dc21   98-3230

On the front cover: The LeTourneau L-1400 is
shown working at the Pittsburgh & Midway (P&M)
Kemmerer Mine in western Wyoming in October
1998. The L-1400 wheel loader is equipped with
a large 33-cubic-yard bucket. It is painted in the
mine's orange color scheme and certainly stands
out in a crowd, not that anyone would miss this
massive 223-ton machine in the first place. *ECO*

On the frontispiece: The Komatsu D575A-2 SD
"Super Dozer" can push thousands of tons of
stone, rock and overburden with its massive 90-
cubic-yard capacity blade and 1,150 flywheel
horsepower. The giant Komatsu makes it look
easy, but that's what you would expect from the
world's largest production crawler dozer. *ECO*

On the title page: The 15-cubic yard capacity
Bucyrus-Erie 280-B electric shovel loads a
235-ton payload WABCO 3200 diesel-electric
drive hauler at Lornex Mining Corporation, Ltd.,
located near Logan Lake, British Columbia,
Canada, in September 1975. *ECO Collection*

On the back cover: *Top:* At 633 tons, the Leibherr
R996 Litronic hydraulic excavator is one of the
most productive front shovels available to the
mining market in the 44-cubic-yard class. Only a
few hydraulic machines built today are larger than
the mighty R996. *Liebherr France. Bottom:* The giant
MEGA CH290 ranks as one of the largest
tractor/trailer combinations of all time. The 290-
ton-plus load capacity trailer is towed by a
Caterpillar 789B tractor. The massive coal hauler,
designed by Magnum, was so large it couldn't be
built under the MEGA facility's roof in Albuquerque,
New Mexico. The final assembly work was
subcontracted to WOTCO in Casper, Wyoming. *ECO*

Edited by Paul Johnson
Designed by Rebecca Allen

Printed in Hong Kong

CONTENTS

ACKNOWLEDGMENTS

It takes input from many individuals to make a book of this kind a reality. I would like to personally thank the following individuals for taking the time and effort in helping me make sure that this subject matter received the attention and respect it so richly deserves. They are David A. Thomas, Bruce K. Malone, John A. W. Bowsher, James P. Rosso, Pete J. Holman, John Ingle, Tom Novak, M. Elaine Barnett, Jeff Hawkinson, Ron Nusbaum, Leo W. Davis, Anthony J. Craig, George Kenyon, Douglas M. Kelley, John Cain, Warren Brisson, Alvin E. Nus, J. Keith Haddock, Doug Knight, Kathy Anderson, William E. Bontemps, Jerry Toelle, William H. Clarke, Bruce Kurschenska, Urs Peyer, Sam Little, Martha Glasgow, Merilee S. Hunt, K. Peter Winkel, W. V. Mateychuk, Jackie Murphy, J. Peter Ahrenkiel, Larry Vargus, Bill Williams, Ed Ward, Mark Dietz, Jay Hillman Jr., Wayne Mynatt, Louis R. Best, William A. Borthwick, Don Boswell, Lee Wary Russell, Tim Tyl, Christine L. Taylor, Bob Heimann, Greg Dundas, Doug Wagner, Craig Jennings, Ken Pauling, Ron Covel, Michael K. Snelling, Bonnie Clemetson, James E. Martens, Steve Brosseau, Jim Harrison, Phil Plotke, Harold Schickel, Kurt Cost, Randy Sandrik, Tom Osborn, Steve Johnson, Rudy Sudrla, Klaus Mayr, and Eileen Grafton.

I would also like to express my sincerest thanks for the support and cooperation of the following companies, many of which I have worked with in a professional capacity over the years. They are the Peabody Group, LeTourneau Inc., Caterpillar Inc., Euclid-Hitachi Heavy Equipment Inc., Komatsu Mining Systems Inc. (KMS), Terex Mining Group, Liebherr Mining Equipment, Bucyrus International, and P & H Mining Equipment.

—*Eric C. Orlemann*

INTRODUCTION

We have often seen large earth-moving machines at work along our roads and highways and in our neighborhoods and cities. But what qualifies equipment as a "Super-Duty Earthmover"? Simply put, these machines are at the top of the food chain when it comes to mining and construction equipment. In their given categories, they are the largest and most powerful heavy-hauling, big digging machines to ever move earth. Some of these creations had long production lives, while others were one-off prototypes that are no longer in existence. All of these machines have one thing in common—the ability to amaze us simply by their size. There are big dump trucks, and then there are really BIG dump trucks.

Over the years, these giant machines, along with the men and women who operate and maintain them, have been the first link in our modern industrialized civilization. The products and services we take for granted on a daily basis, in most cases, started out in the bucket of a large mining shovel. Iron ores, copper, gold, and coal are just a small sampling of the raw materials that must first be removed from the earth, before we can reap the benefits as a society as a whole. From the massive dam and aqueduct projects of the world, to our modern interstate highway system, they all started with these massive construction and mining machines.

In many respects, this book takes up where my first work on the subject, *Giant Earth-Moving Equipment*, published by MBI in 1995, left off. That project dealt with the mammoth excavators and draglines utilized in the mining industry. *Super-Duty* is the second part of the *Giant Earth-Moving Equipment* story. It concentrates on the next groups of large earthmovers, namely the "classic" model lines, such as the haulers, dozers, scrapers, and graders, mainly from the 1950s through the present. But also included is a chapter on modern large excavators that have been released into the marketplace since the publication of *Giant Earth-Moving*, bringing that part of the story up to date as well.

The images throughout this book come from numerous sources. Some are from private collections, while others were hand-picked from many corporate archives. I have personally captured many images over the last few years while doing photographic work for many of these same manufacturers. Since 1989, I have worked at more than 150 mining and large quarry operations in North America, taking photos of new prototypes, current fleets, and older equipment. I can say without hesitation that I still get that thrill of anticipation when going to a mine I have never worked at to photograph these monsters at work. Of course there are the trying days when it rains, snows, or all of the equipment you were supposed to shoot is being repaired. But once the images are captured, the memories and the film are all that remain. I hope by sharing some of these images with you, the reader, that some of the experiences of being in the presence of these giants can be conveyed in some fashion. These machines are truly incredible.

SPECIFICATIONS

The specifications provided throughout this book are all in standard U.S. English SAE weights and measures. Machine and vehicle weights are referred to in tons, which is calculated at 2,000 pounds per short ton. Any metric specifications are identified as such. The average weight of a cubic yard of material is rated at 3,000 pounds. However, there are material density variances, such as a cubic yard of coal, which is rated at about 1,400 to 1,500 pounds. Coal haulers and loaders with extra-capacity dump boxes and buckets have a much higher volume in cubic yards than standard versions, but overall tonnage ratings remain the same. Equipment working with heavier material, such as iron ore at 4,000 to 5,400 pounds a cubic yard, would get lower-volume buckets and dippers. Most terminology in the text is self-explanatory, but following are a few abbreviations that might need further clarification:

Gross horsepower: The output of the engine or motor as installed in the machine, without major accessories connected.

Flywheel horsepower (fhp): The actual horsepower output, with all accessories connected, including the fan, air compressor, generator and hydraulic pump; sometimes referred to as net horsepower.

ROPS: Rollover Protective Structures.

1 REAR DUMP HAULERS

The rear-dump hauler, most commonly referred to as a "dump truck," is one of the most common pieces of earth-moving equipment we see every day. But it is what we don't see that is of the most interest. In large mines and quarries around the world, millions of tons of material are moved daily. To accomplish this, massive off-highway haulers are utilized to move the tons of rock, earth, and other assorted minerals, in the most efficient and productive ways possible.

The building of Boulder Dam, which we now refer to as Hoover Dam, created the need for trucks that were tougher than ordinary over-the-road types then in use. In 1931, Mack Trucks was the first to build a truck that was better suited to the mission at hand, called the super-duty Mack AP. These unique AP haulers, based on the original 1929 AP trucks, were specialty built with 14-cubic yard dump bodies. They utilized chain drive, and for the most part were just beefed-up versions of the company's famous AC "Bulldog" range. The trucks worked out well, but in the end they were still only modified over-the-road models.

The origin of the off-highway hauler is traced directly to a Cleveland, Ohio, firm named the Euclid Road Machinery Company. In late 1933, the company introduced an experimental off-road bottom-dump hauler identified as the Model ZW. From the development of this unit's tractor grew the company's first off-road rear-dump truck in early 1934, the Model Z. Soon to be referred to as a "Trac-Truk," this seven-cubic yard hauler was the first truck built from the ground up and intended strictly for off-road haulage. The Model Z was the forerunner of all Euclid rear-dump trucks, and the industry's first dedicated off-highway hauler.

After World War II, engineering designs developed for military equipment began finding their way into the commercial market. In 1947, Euclid started research into adapting the GM Allison automatic transmissions and torque converters for off-road haulers. Euclid wanted to combine two engines for greater power delivery. The use of two engines, coupled with Allison transmissions, proved viable in tank production. If it worked so well in a tank, why not in a hauler? In 1948, Euclid introduced its Twin-Power concept in a tractor-pulled bottom dump, identified as the 50FDT-102W. By February 1949 things would start to get a bit more interesting, when Euclid unveiled its 34-ton capacity, tandem-drive, 1FFD rear-dump hauler. The 1FFD utilized two GM diesel engines, rated at 380 gross hp combined, each with its own Allison Torqmatic transmission and torque converter. This Twin-Power system allowed synchronized shifting of the two transmissions, which greatly increased the efficiency and productivity of the trucks.

The next big step in hauler development occurred in May 1951, when Euclid introduced its tandem-drive 1LLD model. With Twin-Power, 600 gross hp and a 50-ton capacity, it was the world's largest rear-dump truck, if only for a short time.

Other truck manufacturers would soon follow Euclid's lead. Dart, a manufacturer of trucks since 1903, released its twin-engine,

Caterpillar 797

When the big get even bigger, they graduate into the "ultra" hauler class of mining trucks. Such is the case with Caterpillar's incredible 797 series. With a maximum-rated payload of a staggering 360 tons, it beats the old record of 350 tons set by the Terex 33-19 Titan back in 1974. The 797 is powered by a newly developed Cat 3524B LS EUI, V-24 diesel engine, rated at 3,400 gross hp; like its little brothers, its powertrain is of a mechanical-drive nature. The 797 also rides on big 55/80R63 radial tires mounted on 63-inch rims. The approximate working weight of the Cat 797 fully loaded is 1,230,000 pounds, or 615 tons. The hauler is 47 feet, 7 inches in length, and has a record-setting width of 30 feet. The first prototype Cat 797 started proving ground testing in November 1998. *Caterpillar*

Euclid R-62

The first prototype Euclid 1LLD came off the assembly line in May 1951 and was delivered to Western Contracting Corporation of Sioux City, Iowa, for use at the Fort Randall Dam project in Pickstown, South Dakota. The 1LLD was powered by two Cummins NHRS six-cylinder diesel engines, producing a total output of 600 gross hp, driving the rear tandem axles. Pictured in May 1963 is the last updated LLD tandem-drive model to be designed by the company. This version, an R-62, 5LLD series, was powered by a pair of GM Detroit Diesel 6-110 engines, rated at 672 gross hp and 632 fhp combined. The weight of this model was 118,100 pounds. *ECO Collection*

tandem-drive Model 60, later known as the 75TA, in 1952. This twin-engine hauler, designed by Ralph H. Kress, was powered by two Buda diesel engines, mounted low on the outside chassis frame rails, one on each side, just behind the cab. These engines produced 700 gross hp to carry the truck's 60-ton load. The prototype truck was delivered to Bagdad Copper Corporation's mining operation in Arizona in early 1953. From the beginning, the Buda Super Diesels were not up to the task. Many problems plagued the truck, which caused Bagdad Copper to cancel any further orders for additional units. In 1954 Dart offered the Model 60 as a 75-ton capacity hauler, called the Model 75TA, but it was too late. Interest in the truck's design quickly faded in the mining industry, and with it any hopes of additional Model 60/75TA haulers being built.

Of all the well-known truck builders, Mack Trucks made the best show in the off-highway market. The problem with Mack was its stubborn reliance on chain drive for large quarry and mining trucks. Euclid, the leader at the time, utilized the planetary gear drive axle, which was far superior to the old-style chain-driven wheel system. During the time of the Mack FCSW tandem-drive truck, from 1937 to 1947, the company lost valuable market share to Euclid's FD range of trucks. Mack finally made the move away from chain drive for its off-road haulers with the introduction of the 15-ton capacity LR in 1946 and the 22.5-ton LV in 1948. Both incorporated a single planetary rear-drive axle. In the late 1940s, a tandem-drive, 30-ton LRSW model was also introduced. Other

Western 80

Western Contracting Corporation, of Sioux City, Iowa, decided it needed a massive hauler for use in many of the company's large earth-moving projects. When one of suitable size was not available, they had one built themselves. The 150-ton-capacity Western 80, also referred to as the "Eucnik," was the world's largest hauler when it was built in 1958. The tractor was one of Western's early Euclid 1LLD haulers, which had been previously upgraded with two Cummins Turbo-Diesel engines, rated at 750 gross hp. In 1960, these engines were removed and replaced with two GM Detroit Diesel 12V-71, 12-cylinder units, developing a total of 850 gross hp. The trailer capacity was 80 cubic yards struck and 100 heaped, for a maximum load rating of 300,000 pounds. The overall hauler length was 55 feet, with a 16-foot width. Only one Western 80 was ever constructed. The big hauler started working in 1958 and was taken out of service by 1970. *ECO Collection*

Euclid R-210 Turbine Hauler

The Euclid R-210 has the distinction of being the only mining hauler designed from the ground up with turbine-electric power. The main advantage to this was an exceptionally powerful engine that weighed less than half of its diesel engine counterparts. The hauler was first unveiled in August 1971. The R-210 was powered by a single, compact, Avco-Lycoming TF25 Gas Turbine engine, generating 1,850 gross hp, which was delivered to four electric traction motors, one in each wheel, giving the truck all-wheel drive. Pictured in October 1972 at Euclid's former Laredo Texas Proving Grounds, the R-210 is undergoing further evaluation tests before being delivered to its new home at Bougainville Copper Ltd.'s Panguna Mine on Bougainville Island, Papua New Guinea, in August 1974. The R-210 had a load rating of 210 tons. The truck had an empty weight of 245,000 pounds and carried 665,000 pounds fully loaded. *Doug Kelley*

Mack M-100SX

In the 1960s, Mack Trucks offered a very popular model line of tandem-drive mining haulers in its M-Series. Regular-production models included the M-45SX in 1960, the M-65SX in 1963, the M-70SX in 1965, and the M-75SX in 1970. Often overlooked, though, were the three M-100SX models. Pictured is the first unit, delivered in 1966 to the Babbit Mine of the Reserve Mining Company. Equipped with a Detroit Diesel 12V-149T engine, the hauler produced 800 gross hp. The maximum load capacity was 100 tons. The second unit came off the assembly line in 1967 as a tractor model, intended to pull a 150-ton iron ore trailer. The M-100SX tractor was powered by a Cummins VT12-700-CI diesel engine, rated at 700 gross hp. The third unit was delivered in January 1970 to Hoffman Rigging & Crane Service of New Jersey. Hoffman removed the dump box and converted the truck into a heavy haulage tractor to pull a 700-ton capacity Talbert trailer. It was powered by the same Detroit Diesel engine found in the first unit, with horsepower increased to 1,000 gross, making it one of the most powerful prime movers in the world at the time. *Mack Trucks Historical Museum*

popular tandem-drive Mack trucks soon followed, including the 34-ton LRVSW in late 1951 and the 40-ton LYSW in 1958.

The two major quarry and mining truck manufacturers during the 1950s were, of course, Euclid, the undisputed leader at the time, and Dart. But while Euclid and Dart were keeping an eye on each other, the next major advancement in the off-road hauler was about to take place. This time it would be made by LeTourneau-Westinghouse. Headquartered in Peoria, Illinois, LeTourneau-Westinghouse (L-W) was formed in 1953, after Westinghouse Air Brake Company purchased the earth-moving equipment manufacturing part of R. G. LeTourneau's business. In December 1956, the company's first prototype two-axle, rigid- frame, rear-dump hauler rolled out the factory doors—the revolutionary LW-30 Haulpak. The 30-ton capacity LW-30 was the design creation of Ralph H. Kress, the former executive vice president and general manager of Dart Trucks. Innovative in

design, the LW-30 was the first to use the "Hydrair" oil-air suspension system, which Kress also pioneered. Other notable design features included an offset cab and a triangular sloping dump box. Officially released in 1957, the Haulpak line of quarry and mining trucks would soon become the industry design benchmark.

Up until this time, all of the accepted heavy-duty, off-road haulers used mechanical-drive systems. These vehicles utilized an engine, a transmission, manual or automatic, and planetary gear drive axles. But during the 1950s, a new technology was starting to emerge that would compete with the traditional accepted drivetrains of the day. This innovation was the diesel-electric powertrain.

Diesel-electric drive technology for the earth-moving industry was championed by R. G. LeTourneau after his sale of the earth-moving equipment portion of his company. Between April 30, 1953, and May 1, 1958, R. G. LeTourneau agreed to a mora-

torium on competing against LeTourneau-Westinghouse in the production of earth-moving equipment. During this time, LeTourneau began to perfect his electric wheel traction motors for use in earth-moving equipment. The first practical application of this electric-drive system in an off-highway, rear-dump hauler was the experimental LeTourneau TR-60 "Trolley-Dump," unveiled at the company's Longview plant in Texas in June 1959.

Codevelopment of the TR-60 started in 1958 with R. G. LeTourneau and the Anaconda Company, in conjunction with its Mining Research Department. The purpose of the TR-60 was to evaluate the electric truck concept in open-pit mining at Anaconda's Berkeley Pit in Butte, Montana. After a delay in the start of testing due to an eight-month strike at the Berkeley Pit, the TR-60 officially started working in April 1960. The drivetrain of the original articulated TR-60 consisted of a Cummins "Super-Diesel" engine, rated at 335 gross hp, which was direct-coupled to AC and DC generators. These supplied power to four electric traction motors, one in each wheel-hub assembly. When the TR-60 was attached to overhead electric trolley cables by front-mounted pantograph arms, the electric wheel motors produced 1,600 gross hp and 1,242 net, or actual, horsepower. The diesel engine came into play when the hauler was disconnected from the trolley line, powering the generators, which maneuvered the truck in areas where the overhead lines were not available, such as the dump site. The diesel engine supplied power to the braking and steering systems at all times, even when attached to the overhead trolley lines. The TR-60 was rated as a 60-ton capacity hauler, but during the early testing period, the truck almost always averaged 65 tons per load. Later in the testing of the TR-60, an additional 335-gross-hp diesel engine was added, parallel-mounted in the front, driving the generator. This was needed to help improve the truck's poor slow-speed maneuvering when it was loaded and separated from the trolley electric power supply. This engine up-grade helped boost the truck's payload capacity to 75 tons.

Unit Rig & Equipment Company of Tulsa, Oklahoma, a manufacturer of oil-drilling equipment since 1935, had what it took to build a diesel-electric drive, rear-dump hauler, for use in open pit mining operations. Its extensive experience with high-horsepower diesel engines and electrically driven

Euclid R-170
One of Euclid's best-selling large-capacity haulers over the years has been its diesel-electric drive R-170 model. Introduced in late 1974, it is still in Euclid's current product line as of 1998, though much refined and updated. When introduced, the hauler had a maximum payload rating of 170 tons. Today's R-170 has a payload capacity of 183 tons. A 1,600-gross-hp and 1,519-fhp 16-cylinder Cummins KTA50-C diesel is standard, with an optional 1,492-fhp Detroit Diesel engine available. Optional 1,800-gross-hp versions of both engines can also be ordered. The maximum loaded weight of the R-170 is 615,000 pounds. Pictured in mid-1974 is the prototype R-170. *ECO Collection*

Euclid R-190

Euclid introduced its popular 190-ton-capacity R-190 hauler in 1986. In 1996, the company released an updated version of the R-190. Most notable is the revised front end of the hauler. As in the original model, two engine choices are available. The customer has the choice of a Cummins K1800E, or a Detroit Diesel 16V-149TIB engine; both are rated at 1,800 gross hp and 1,650 fhp, with optional 2,000-gross-units available from both engine

suppliers. The hauler has a weight of 280,537 pounds empty and 685,000 pounds fully loaded. The maximum capacity for this R-190 model is 202 tons. Euclid trucks are usually shipped painted in "Hi-Lite" green for North American customers and in "Volvo" yellow for the rest of the world. But customers have the final say as to the paint scheme on their trucks, such as this yellow R-190 working at a coal mine in southern Indiana. *ECO*

Euclid R-260

Euclid-Hitachi officially introduced its R-260 hauler at the September 1996 MINExpo in Las Vegas, Nevada. The R-260 looks a bit different from other haulers in its class, with its distinctive dual front steps and landings by the air cleaners. The big "Euc" gets its power from a Detroit Diesel/MTU S-4000 DDEC engine, rated at 2,500 gross hp and 2,390 fhp. The weight of the R-260 is 327,699 pounds empty, and 850,800 pounds loaded. The maximum payload rating is 262 tons. Pictured at a mine site in Ely, Nevada, in November 1996, the prototype R-260 gets ready to start its long-term field testing program. *ECO*

machinery systems, as they related to drilling rigs, would prepare them well for the ambitious project. On January 27, 1960, Unit Rig unveiled its first experimental prototype truck—the Lectra Haul M-64 Ore Hauler. The M-64 was a 64-ton capacity, articulated-steered, rear-dump hauler; it was

Euclid R-220

In 1995, Euclid delivered a special fleet of R-220 haulers to the Palabora Copper Mine at Phalaborwa, in eastern South Africa. These trucks were equipped with large front-mounted pantographs for use with the mine's overhead electric trolley system. The trucks manually hook up to the trolley wires as they start to climb the long steep grades out of the pit. The overhead electric lines supply current to the electric-drive system of the truck, which helps take the strain off the diesel engine and improves fuel economy. Engine choices for the R-220 are either a Cummins K2000E diesel, rated at 2,000 gross hp and 1,854 fhp, or a Detroit Diesel 16V-149TIB, rated at 2,000 gross hp and 1,850 fhp. The maximum payload capacity is 217 tons. The R-220 was originally referred to as the R-190 Plus. *Euclid-Hitachi*

the first to use the General Electric motorized wheel system for off-road, earth-moving applications. The hauler was powered by a single Cummins VT-12-BI diesel engine, rated at 700 gross hp and 630 flywheel hp. This supplied power to the main generator, which drove the GE electric wheel motors, mounted within the rim assemblies at all four corners. After the early factory testing of the M-64 was completed, the unit was shipped to the Hanna Mining Company for testing at its iron ore mine in Minnesota. But after some especially grueling hauling application tests, Unit Rig felt the articulated design was not up to working in open pit mining operations. On the other hand, the diesel-electric GE drive system had demonstrated impressive performance characteristics.

The technical information gained with the experimental M-64 led directly to Unit Rig's next truck, the Lectra Haul M-85. Gone was the articulated steering chassis, now replaced by a rigid frame. Looking much like the modern haulers of the day, the M-85 was diesel-electric drive, utilizing GE traction

Dart DE930
The Dart 120-ton-capacity DE930 is an often overlooked model in the company's history. Designed from the ground up as a diesel-electric drive truck, it was supposed to mark a turning point in the history of Dart hauler technology. The company had offered electric-driven models before, but for the most part these were conversion packages used on trucks that were first designed with mechanical powertrains. The DE930 was first introduced in late 1971 and was powered by a GM Detroit Diesel 12V-149T engine, rated at 1,000 gross hp and 900 fhp. The electric-drive system was supplied by GE and utilized traction wheel motors. The DE930, along with its big brother introduced in late 1972, the 150-ton-capacity DE940, were not successful in the marketplace. Their diesel-electric drivetrains were just too unreliable and eventually forced the company to abandon the concept for hauler applications. But the overall look and basic design of the DE930 would eventually shape future Dart models. *ECO Collection*

Unit Rig Lectra Haul M-200
Probably no single truck had a bigger impact on the large hauler market than Unit Rig & Equipment Company's Lectra Haul M-200. The Tulsa, Oklahoma-based company was the first to release a 200-ton-capacity, diesel-electric drive production truck to the mining industry. The M-200 hauler was first introduced by Unit Rig in late 1968, with the first units shipped from the factory in September 1969 to Kaiser Resources, in Sparwood, British Columbia, for use in its open-pit coal mine. The first trucks were powered by an 8-cylinder, GM EMD 8-645-E4 diesel locomotive engine, producing 1,650 gross hp and 1,500 fhp. Later, a 12-cylinder, GM EMD 12-645-E4 engine, with a power output of 2,475 gross hp and 2,250 fhp was made available. Severe tire wear problems plagued the first trucks delivered equipped with 36.00-51, 50PR size tires. This problem was solved with the availability of 40.00-57, 60PR tires. The prototype M-200 is pictured here being loaded by the first P&H 2800 electric mining shovel in 1969. It carries the mine's equipment number of 309 (which was later changed to 313). A total of 120 M-200 haulers were eventually put into service worldwide. *ECO Collection*

motors in the rear drive wheels. The engine of choice was the Cummins VT-12-700, rated at 700 gross hp. With an 85-ton payload rating, it was one of the largest two-axle haulers available at that time. The M-85 was no experimental pipe dream, but was in fact the first true production diesel-electric drive, rigid-frame, rear-dump truck for mining applications. The first M-85 was delivered to Kennecott Copper's Chino Mine in New Mexico in July 1963; suddenly Unit Rig Lectra Haul trucks were a force to be reckoned with in the mining equipment industry.

Caterpillar, the powerhouse earth-moving equipment manufacturer, was poised to enter the off-road truck market. Development of a 35-ton capacity, mechanical-drive, power-shift, rear-dump hauler was put into high gear in 1961, with the first model, the Caterpillar 769, to be introduced in 1962. While the prototype testing program of the 769 hauler was being conducted in 1962, Ralph Kress, formerly of LeTourneau-Westinghouse, took the position of manager of truck development at Caterpillar. He initiated the development of its electric-drive hauler program, and kept an eye on the 769 mechanical-drive truck. His efforts resulted in the prototype 75-ton capacity Model 779; the 100-ton side-dump, three-axle 783; and the mammoth 240-ton bottom-dump 786 coal hauler, all unveiled in 1965.

All of the truck programs were designed concurrently, so the haulers could share many of the same components. All were powered by Cat Diesel D348, V-12 engines, rated at 1,000 gross hp and 960 fhp, attached to Caterpillar-designed electric-drive

Unit Rig Lectra Haul Mark 36

Even though the Lectra Haul M-200 hauler was Unit Rig's largest-capacity truck in the late 1960s and the 1970s, it was the 170-ton-capacity Mark 36 model that was the company's real breadwinner. The Mark 36 became the hauler backbone for numerous large-scale mining operations throughout the world. It didn't matter if copper, gold, iron ore, or coal was being mined, the Mark 36 was there. In the later models, this diesel-electric drive hauler was powered by either a Cummins KTTA50-C1600, or a Detroit Diesel 16V149TI diesel engine, both rated at 1,600 gross hp and 1,454 fhp. Unit Rig shipped its first Mark 36 in August 1972. Originally conceived of as a 150-ton capacity hauler, it soon became evident in early testing that the truck could easily handle 170 tons. The total number of Mark 36 trucks built by Unit Rig was 685. *ECO Collection*

Unit Rig Lectra Haul MT-4000

Unit Rig's offering in the supercompetitive 240-ton class of haul trucks was its Lectra Haul MT-4000. Originally released in 1988, the MT-4000 evolved from a series of trucks, starting with the MT-1900 in 1984, the MT-2050 in 1986 and the MT-2120 in 1987. The 240-ton capacity MT-4000 was offered with three engine choices, the largest of them a Detroit Diesel 20V-149TIB, 20-cylinder engine, rated at 2,500 gross hp and 2,334 fhp. The empty weight of the hauler is 309,268 pounds with a 789,268-pound maximum weight. The MT-4000 rides on 40.00-57,68PR size tires; the length of the unit is 43 feet, with a 23-foot width. Today, Unit Rig is part of Terex Mining Group. *Terex*

systems. But the performance reliability of the electric-drive system was in question. Some people within Caterpillar felt the electric-drive concept should be abandoned entirely, and engineering resources should be directed toward the creation of a power-shift automatic transmission for use in a 50-ton hauler. In the end, the mechanical-drive backers within the company won out. After Kress retired from Caterpillar in 1969, the diesel-electric program was canceled. From that point on, all of Cat's haulers would be of a conventional mechanical-drive nature.

The need for more powerful engines in the mid-1960s resulted in substantial but ultimately misguided efforts to develop the use of gas turbine engines in haul trucks. The advantages of turbine engines were their high power outputs, lower overall engine weight than their diesel counterparts, high reliability, and long service and rebuild intervals. The big downside was their fuel

Unit Rig Lectra Haul MT-4000

This special Lectra Haul MT-4000, working in 1992 at Boliden Mineral's Apirsa Aznalcollar Mine, near Seville, Spain, is equipped with supercooling dual radiators with parallel fans, as is the rest of the mine's Unit Rig fleet. This helps the big haulers keep their cool in the area's high ambient temperatures, which often exceed 120 degrees Fahrenheit. These trucks are powered by Detroit Diesel 16V-149TIB engines, rated at 2,200 gross hp and 2,054 fhp. The MT-4000 is being loaded by a 25-cubic yard capacity Demag H285S front shovel, weighing in at 369 tons. *Terex*

economy. A turbine burned almost twice as much fuel as a diesel engine.

Unit Rig was the first to field experimental turbine trucks in 1965, with two modified Lectra Haul M-100 haulers. One M-100 was equipped with a 1,200-gross-hp GE LM-100 gas turbine. The second M-100 was supplied with 1,100-gross-hp IH Solar Saturn gas turbine. WABCO, the new corporate name of LeTourneau-

Westinghouse, tested five 120A Haulpak trucks fitted with IH Solar Saturn gas turbines in 1969. Tests of all of these trucks were somewhat encouraging, but there were numerous drawbacks, which indicated that adapting turbine power to existing truck platforms caused more problems than it solved. Most of these test trucks were eventually returned to their original diesel-electric drivetrain layouts.

Euclid, Inc., under the ownership of White Motor Corp., started testing the turbine engine concept in a specially converted R-105 articulated hauler in the Mesabi Iron Range of Minnesota in 1970. The engine in the test truck was a 1,100-gross-hp Avco-Lycoming TF14 gas turbine, de-rated to 1,000 gross hp. After the test program was finished, the R-105 was returned with its original drivetrain. Test

Unit Rig Lectra Haul MT-4400

Announced at the end of 1994, the Lectra Haul MT-4400 was officially released for sale in 1995, with the first fleet going to Powder River Coal Company's Caballo Mine, in the Powder River Basin coal area of Gillette, Wyoming. When the trucks were first released, they were initially rated as 280-ton haulers. But the 44-inch-wide tires around which the truck was designed never materialized. Now the truck is rated as a 260-ton unit.

The MT-4400 is powered by a Detroit Diesel/MTU 16V-396TE engine, rated at 2,467 gross hp and 2,287 fhp. The vehicle has an empty weight of 344,572 pounds and weighs 865,000 pounds fully loaded. The overall length is 45 feet, 7 inches, and the width is 24 feet, 2 inches. Other than the early tire wear problems, these trucks have been just about as bulletproof as you can get with this type of a giant hauler. *ECO*

results and engineering knowledge were gained and used when the company's radical new hauler—the turbine-electric drive Euclid R-210—was finalized. The 210-ton capacity truck was powered by a very compact Avco-Lycoming TF25 gas turbine engine, rated at 1,850 gross hp. The R-210 housed the engine, not in the front of the truck, but between the frame rails, behind the operator's main deck, just in front of the rear axle housing. This supplied power to the generator, which in turn drove the traction motors—one per dual tire wheel assembly.

The R-210 made its world debut at the October 1971 American Mining Congress show in Las Vegas, Nevada. In tests at the plant and at Euclid's Laredo Texas Proving Grounds during 1972 and 1973, the R-210 performed exceptionally well. Things looked bright for the project until the oil crisis began. Overnight, fuel prices went through the roof, and just as fast, the R-210 turbine project fell through the floor. The minor problem of the truck's poor fuel economy caused the whole R-210 program to go into cardiac arrest. The prototype truck eventually found a home at Bougainville Copper's Panguna Mine in Papua New Guinea, in 1974. Even though two R-210 trucks were planned, only one was assembled. Parts

Peerless VCON 3006

The Peerless VCON 3006, a 250-ton hauler, was designed by the Peerless Manufacturing Company of Dallas, Texas, to be the world's largest mining hauler. Work started on the development of the hauler in April 1970. Fourteen months later, the finished truck was delivered to the Pima Copper Mine in Arizona, June 1971. Originally released as the VCON 2606, the nomenclature was changed to 3006 because the engine specified for installation in the truck had multiple horsepower ratings. The engine was the four-stroke, 12-cylinder, Alco 251-12E diesel locomotive engine, with power ratings ranging from 2,600 to 3,000 gross hp. Initially, the power output was placed at 2,600 gross hp, but it was soon upgraded to 3,000 gross hp and 2,790 fhp. Power was supplied to six GE electric traction motors, one in each of the four rear wheels and one in each of the two outside front wheels. With a full 250-ton load, the 350,000-pound VCON 3006 weighed in at 850,000 pounds. The empty truck was a bit on the heavy side, due to the redundant testing equipment installed on the prototype machine to compare compatibility of different components. The length of the unit was 43 feet and the overall width was a very wide 28 feet. *ECO Collection*

Peerless/Marion VCON 3006

Marion Power Shovel Company acquired the rights to the VCON division of Peerless in May 1973 and diverted research funds away from the hauler to actively pursue the VCON V-250 Dozer project. In 1976, the Russian Coal Ministry indicated an interest in the 3006 hauler concept. A presentation was submitted to the Russians and to Sumitomo Heavy Industries, on a joint effort plan by Marion and Sumitomo to produce a 300-ton-capacity version of the 3006. In the end, the Russians chose the Lectra Haul M-200 over the VCON, to be loaded by Marion 204-M Superfront Shovels, which were to be built by Sumitomo. When Dresser Industries purchased the Marion Power Shovel Company in 1977, all development work in the VCON hauler ended. Only one VCON 3006 (2606) was ever produced. *ECO Collection*

LeTourneau-Westinghouse LW-30

The turning point in the design history of the off-road hauler industry would be the truck pictured here in December 1956, the LeTourneau-Westinghouse LW-30. This LW-30 was the very first Haulpak truck built, with most of the key design elements credited to Ralph Kress, whom many consider the father of the modern mining truck. Key features of this truck design included an offset cab, Hydair air-hydraulic suspension, and a triangular, sloping dump box to lower the center of gravity. The LW-30 was powered by an eight-cylinder Cummins diesel engine, rated at 375 gross hp. The payload capacity was 30 tons. This truck series became the Model 32 in 1959. *ECO Collection*

WABCO Haulpak 200B

The Haulpak 200B was the largest diesel-electric drive, three-axle, tractor/trailer rear-dump hauler ever offered on the market. Outside suppliers in the past had produced 150-ton versions, but this was the first time a manufacturer had produced its own 200-ton-capacity design. The top engine choice was the 16-cylinder GM 16V-149T diesel engine, producing 1,600 gross hp and 1,440 fhp. Power was supplied to the rear axle of the tractor and the axle of the dump trailer, making the unit four-wheel drive. The maximum loaded weight of the 200B was 675,000 pounds. The overall length was 55 feet, with a 20-foot width. The 200B prototype unit first went to work in October 1969 at the Duval Copper Mine, near Tucson, Arizona, for field evaluations. Pictured is the first production unit of the 200B at U.S. Steel's Mountain Iron Mine in Minnesota, in October 1971. The 200B was developed from the experimental 160A from November 1965. *KMS*

WABCO Haulpak 3200

Starting in September 1971, WABCO began testing the first of six Haulpak 3200 prototype diesel-electric tandem-drive 200-ton haulers, powered by a two-stroke, 12-cylinder, GM EMD 12-645-E4 diesel locomotive engine. Even though this engine was rated at 2,475 gross hp, it was de-rated to 2,000 gross hp and 1,800 fhp. With a full 200-ton load, the 3200 had a gross weight of 717,000 pounds. The length was 50 feet, 6 inches, with a 22-foot, 7-inch width. The 3200 rode on 10-size, 33.00-51,42PR tires. In early 1975, the Haulpak 3200 was released in an upgraded B version. The GM EMD locomotive engine remained the same, except that the horsepower output was increased to the full rating of 2,475 gross hp and 2,250 fhp at only 900 rpm. The load capacity was also increased to 235 tons, with the use of larger 36.00-51,42PR-size tires. Shown here working in April 1973 at Kennecott Copper's Ray Mine (now operated by ASARCO) in Arizona, is one of the early 3200 test trucks. *KMS*

for the second unit were used to repair the first after a collision in March 1975. The R-210 was eventually pulled from active service in the late 1970s.

When the promises of turbine power failed to materialize in the late 1960s, manufacturers looked to the only other high-horsepower source available, the diesel locomotive engine. These engines produced massive amounts of horsepower at very low RPM, and were very reliable, almost bulletproof in some cases. The one big drawback to these engines was their weight. The locomotive engines were extremely heavy when compared to other higher-revving diesels in use.

The first production hauler to have a locomotive engine installed as standard equipment was the Unit Rig Lectra Haul M-200, introduced in late 1968. During the 1960s, Unit Rig never shied away from pushing the boundaries of large truck powertrain applications, and this model was no exception. The 200-ton capacity M-200 had a choice of two diesel engine options—a 1,650-gross-hp, 8-cylinder, or a 2,475-gross-hp, 12-cylinder. Once some early tire problems were worked out in the

WABCO Haulpak 3200B

Pictured in August 1976, this WABCO 3200B is the largest-capacity version ever built. The maximum payload had been increased to 260 tons without bed liners when the larger-ply-rated 36.00-51,50PR tires were specified. Horsepower and engine specifications remained unchanged. The last version of this truck had an empty weight of 365,000 pounds and a fully loaded weight of 885,000 pounds. The length had also increased to 54 feet, with a 24-foot width. The 3200B would remain in production until economic conditions forced its withdrawal from the market in the early 1980s. Around 48 units were produced in the 3200 series production run. *KMS*

Komatsu Haulpak 830E

Announced in late 1987, and officially unveiled in April 1988 as the Dresser Haulpak 830E, this large truck was the best-selling 240-ton-capacity-class, diesel-electric drive hauler in the industry. Today's 830E, which is now built by Komatsu, is rated with a maximum payload capacity of 255 tons. Power is supplied by a 16-cylinder, MTU/DDC 16V-4000 engine rated at 2,500 gross hp and 2,409 fhp. It puts this power to the ground through large 40.00-57-size tires which carry an empty truck weight of 340,398 pounds and a fully loaded weight of 850,650 pounds. The overall length is 44 feet, 4 inches, with a width of 24 feet. This hauler first started development as the 780E, but was changed to the 830E before the first truck was produced. *ECO*

Komatsu Haulpak 930E

In May 1995, Komatsu officially introduced the latest heavy hauler to the mining industry—the giant Haulpak 930E. What makes the 930E stand out is not so much its capacity, which at 310 tons was massive, but its use of an AC electric-drive motor system. Before the 930E, diesel-electric-driven trucks used DC traction motors. The high-efficiency AC drive system, developed by GE, contains many of the advanced control systems and components first developed for their AC diesel-electric-driven locomotives. The 930E is powered by a MTU/DDC 16V-4000 diesel engine, rated at 2,700 gross hp and 2,500 fhp. Pictured in September 1996, working at the ASARCO Ray Mine, near Hayden, Arizona, this 930E was the third hauler built. It is being loaded by an electric-powered, 44-cubic yard Demag H485SE front shovel. *ECO*

early trucks, the M-200 was one tough hunk of iron.

In early 1970, KW-Dart tried its hand at building a 200-ton capacity, diesel-electric drive hauler, powered by a locomotive engine called the DE-2991. This experimental hauler was powered by an 1,800-gross-hp, GE FDL-8, eight-cylinder, locomotive diesel. While the truck was on trials at Kaiser Steel's Eagle Mountain Mine in California, some of the DE-2991 hauler's design shortcomings were making themselves known. The weight of the engine was overloading the front steering wheels, causing massive amounts of tire scrubbing and wear problems. The Dart was just not up to the task.

WABCO had better luck with its 200-ton hauler. The first three-axle WABCO 3200 Haulpak truck entered service in 1971, equipped with a 2,475-gross-hp, 12-cylinder, locomotive diesel, which was also utilized in the Lectra Haul M-200. The first models produced of the 3200 were rated at 200 tons capacity, which was later increased to 235 tons, and then 260 tons in the 3200B version. With about 48 units of the big tandem-drive truck built, it was considered a moderate success for a hauler of its proportions.

While WABCO was developing the 3200 project, another manufacturer, Peerless Manufacturing Company of Dallas, Texas, was about to enter the off-road hauler market with a radically designed concept truck called the VCON 2606. Peerless, a manufacturer of centrifugal separators and pulsation dampeners in the natural gas transmission and petrochemical industry, formed its Vehicle Constructors division

Terex 33-15

General Motors' Terex Division released its first diesel-electric drive hauler, the 33-15 series, in May 1971. Built at GM's EMD plant in London, Ontario, Canada, it would be the first in a line of very successful large-capacity rear dumps. The original 150-ton-capacity Terex 33-15 model was produced from 1971 to 1974. The upgraded 170-ton version, the 33-15B, was in production from 1975 to 1981. After GM sold Terex in 1981 to IBH, GM retained ownership of the Canadian-built haulers, changing the product name to Diesel Division Titan trucks. An even larger two-axle hauler was planned by Terex for introduction in 1980, the 200-ton-capacity 33-17. But because of the worsening economic climate of the time, the project was canceled. The 33-15 was powered by a GM Detroit Diesel 16V-149TI engine, rated at 1,600 gross hp and 1,445 fhp. With a full load, the truck weighed in at 535,000 pounds. *ECO Collection*

Terex 33-19 Titan

In October 1974, at the American Mining Congress show in Las Vegas, Nevada, Terex unveiled its massive 350-ton, capacity 33-19 Titan hauler, the world's largest dump truck. It was manufactured at the Diesel Division, General Motors of Canada, Ltd., in London, Ontario. Power to move such a truck was supplied by a two-stroke, 16-cylinder, 169-liter, GM EMD 16-645-E4 diesel locomotive engine, rated at 3,300 gross hp and 3,000 fhp at only 900 rpm. This powered the rear tandem axles through four electric GM D79CFA traction motors mounted in the axles. The 10 wheels carried the largest tires then available, size 40.00-57,60PR(E4). After the show, the Titan was moved to its first home at Kaiser Steel's Eagle Mountain Mine in southern California. Pictured is the Titan in March 1976. *ECO Collection*

Komatsu Haulpak 930E

When the Komatsu Haulpak 930E was introduced, it was equipped with the world's largest off-highway radial truck tire, the Bridgestone 48-95R57 VELS. But early tire wear concerns called for an even larger size. Again, it would be Bridgestone that supplied the rubber with the new superwide 50-90R57 series radial tires. These tires would also help increase the 930E's payload capacity to 320 tons. Fully loaded, the truck weighs in at 1,059,000 pounds. Pictured in December 1997, this 930E is working in the harsh winter conditions of northern Alberta, at Syncrude's oil sand operations, just north of Fort McMurray. *KMS*

Terex 33-19 Titan

All dimensions of the Terex 33-19 Titan were huge. The length of the hauler was 66 feet, and it had a width of 25 feet, 7 inches. The empty weight of the truck was 520,000 pounds, and fully loaded it weighed 1,220,400 pounds, or 610 tons. The top speed of the Titan was 30 miles per hour with a full payload on a level haul road. To help it maneuver and to limit the tendency of the unit to understeer, the rear axle had the limited ability to steer with the front wheels when the hauler was in motion. In November 1978, the 33-19 started operations at its new home at Kaiser Resources' Balmer Mine near Sparwood, British Columbia, located in the Kootenay region of the Canadian Rocky Mountains. Pictured in June 1984, the 33-19 is painted in the colors of Westar Mining, owners of the Balmer Mine at the time. *Bruce Kurschenska*

in early 1970. The company had hopes of expanding the company's interest in supplying large earth-moving equipment to the open pit mining industry. The hauler was originally designated the VCON 2606, which referred to 2,600 horsepower and six driving wheels. But shortly after the truck was commissioned in 1971, the nomenclature was changed to 3006, meaning 3,000 horsepower and six driving wheels. The 250-ton capacity, diesel-electric drive VCON was powered by a big Alco, 12-cylinder, locomotive engine, with a maximum power rating of 3,000 gross hp. Key features of the hauler were its walking beam frame, liquid spring suspension, and eight single independent tire mounts, with GE traction wheel motors in six of them. It was an engineering tour de force.

The VCON 3006 was shipped to the Pima Copper Mine in Arizona, in June 1971. After long-term component testing was completed, the truck was removed from the mine site in November 1972 and returned to the Peerless plant for a complete teardown and design inspection of all major systems, to ready the concept truck in preproduction form. But it was soon evident that Peerless had bitten off more than it could chew with such an ambitious project, so an outside partner was sought. Negotiations between Peerless and Marion Power Shovel Company commenced in November 1972 and concluded in May 1973. Marion acquired the rights to purchase and market VCON equipment from Peerless, and in June 1974, the company decided to exercise its option to purchase the VCON division outright. Marion then diverted research away from the hauler program to actively pursue the VCON V-250 Dozer project. When Dresser Industries bought the Marion Power Shovel Company in 1977, all development work in the VCON hauler ended.

The last hauler program to be designed around a locomotive engine was the massive three-axle Terex 33-19 Titan truck from 1974. This giant 350-ton capacity hauler utilized a GM EMD, 16-cylinder diesel, rated at 3,300 gross hp. This was the largest locomotive-type engine application ever introduced in an off-highway hauler. The 33-19 did not use wheel motors. The Titan's four traction motors were mounted inside the rear drive axles, two per unit. The Titan was literally designed around the EMD engine and its 40.00x57 size tires. The truck's rear tandem-drive axles also had the limited ability to turn with the front wheels,

Diesel Division Titan 33-19

After GM sold its Terex Division in 1981, the Terex name was removed from the front of the 33-19 and replaced with "TITAN," the new hauler line name of the GM Diesel Division in Canada. The mine where the hauler worked was also going through ownership changes: The 33-19 was first delivered to Kaiser Resources in 1978, but B.C. Coal, Ltd., took over operations in 1980. The name changed to the Westar Mining Company in 1983, and the truck was repainted in Westar company colors the following year. It would carry these colors into 1990, when a cracked rear axle housing ended the truck's working days. The hauler was officially removed from the active truck fleet roster in 1991. Today the truck is on permanent display in the town of Sparwood, donated by Teck Corporation, which bought the Balmer Mine in December 1992 after Westar went into bankruptcy. The Balmer operation has since been renamed the Elkview Coal Corporation. The 33-19 is pictured in 1988 transporting a 242-ton O&K RH120C backhoe to a new work site on the other side of the Balmer pit. Only one Terex/Diesel Division Titan 33-19 was ever constructed. *Bruce Kurschenska*

which helped reduce the hauler's tendency to understeer. After the truck was shown at the American Mining Congress show in Las Vegas, Nevada, in October 1974, it was shipped in December to Kaiser Steel's Eagle Mountain iron ore mine in California. The truck officially started working in March 1975. In late 1978, the hauler was shipped up to Kaiser Resources' Balmer mine in British Columbia, Canada, where it would work until 1990, after which a severely cracked rear axle housing would end the Titan's working days. Sales of other 33-19 haulers were pending in 1981, but the worldwide financial recession of the early 1980s caused all hopes of selling any more trucks to quickly evaporate.

Starting in the 1980s, the industry reached its next milestone—a production two-axle hauler over the 200-ton capacity range. Even though a few haulers in the past had matched or bettered this figure, they were either three-axle configurations or were experimental prototypes. The truck that broke the barrier was the Wiseda KL-2450.

In 1980, William Seldon Davis, formerly of KENDAVIS Industries, formed his own company, Wiseda Ltd., with the intention of building a better large-capacity hauler. Davis was no stranger to the off-highway truck business. He was part of the family that owned and operated Unit Rig Equipment, makers of the Lectra Haul line of trucks. His new operation, Wiseda, an acronym of Davis' name, released its first KL-2450 "King of the Lode" hauler in 1982. This was the industry's first-production, two-axle, 220-ton hauler. Then again in 1985, Wiseda released the industry's first 240-ton unit. Big accomplishments from a relatively small company at the time.

During the 1980s, Caterpillar began to flex its muscles in the large mining truck market. The company slowly released its haul trucks to proven tonnage categories in the off-highway truck market. Starting in late 1984, the company began its assault on the large mining truck market with the 150-ton capacity model 785, followed by the 195-ton model 789 in 1986. The 789 series in particular continues to dominate the 190- to 200-ton class of trucks in the industry.

Haulers kept growing in capacity and complexity in the 1990s. Some of the larger offerings included the 195-ton Caterpillar 789B/C; the 205-ton Komatsu 730E; the 205-ton Unit Rig MT-3700B; the 215-ton Liebherr T-252; the 217-ton Euclid R-220; the 240-ton Caterpillar 793C; the 250-ton Liebherr T-262; the 255-ton Komatsu 830E; the 260-ton Unit Rig MT-4400; and the 262-ton Euclid R-260. Of these trucks, the Caterpillar 793/B/C series of mining haulers, introduced in 1990, was the most popular—and by a wide margin. With its mechanical drivetrain, it proved that not all large-capacity mining trucks needed to be of an electric-drive type.

Ultra-haulers

In the mid-1990s, a new breed of mining trucks, far larger than their predecessors, had begun to appear in the marketplace. This new group, unofficially identified as "ultra-haulers," are mining trucks with payloads at and above 300 tons capacity. Though the industry has seen trucks this large before with the three-axle, 350-ton

LeTourneau Titan T-2240
The largest hauler built by LeTourneau was The 240-ton-capacity T-2240. The first two units were delivered in March and April 1990 to Westar Mining Company, British Columbia, Canada, for field evaluation. The standard power source was a 16-cylinder, Detroit Diesel 16V-149TI engine, rated at 2,200 fhp. The weight was 336,900 pounds empty and 816,900 pounds loaded. The hauler rode on 40.00-57,68PR-size tires, and overall length was 47 feet, with a 22-foot width. In early 1995, the T-2240 hauler model was removed from LeTourneau's product line. Only four T-2240 haulers were ever built. *LeTourneau, Inc.*

LeTourneau Titan T-2200
In January 1985, Marathon LeTourneau of Longview, Texas, purchased the Titan hauler line from the Diesel Division, General Motors of Canada, Ltd. Initially, the truck was known as the LeTourneau Titan 33-15C and was little changed from the GM version. But soon after the purchase, LeTourneau started revamping the entire hauler line. The end result of this effort was the introduction of the new T-2000 TITAN series of haul trucks in September 1996. The truck line consisted of haulers ranging in capacity from 170 to 200 tons, with a 240-ton version added later. The 200-ton-capacity T-2200 was available with either a Cummins or Detroit Diesel engine, rated at 2,000 fhp. The weight was 316,900 pounds empty and 716,900 pounds fully loaded. In early 1994, the Titan name was officially retired from use on the haulers. Pictured is a 200-ton-capacity Titan T-2200 hauler, working in 1996 at the ASARCO Mission mine in Arizona. *ECO*

capacity Terex 33-19 Titan in 1974, the ultra-haulers are all two-axle designs. The ultra-haulers all use high-revving diesel engines, rather than the heavy, low-revving locomotive diesel designs. They also incorporate the latest tire and wheel designs, essential when carrying such mammoth loads on only two axles.

The first of this new generation of haulers was the Komatsu Haulpak 930E, introduced in 1995. The 930E represented the most technologically advanced Haulpak truck ever built. The Haulpak truck line over the years has displayed many corporate names, such as LeTourneau-Westinghouse, WABCO, Dresser, Komatsu-Dresser, and now finally Komatsu. Through all of these company name changes, buyouts, and joint ventures, the Haulpak product line has endured and grown. The largest Haulpak, as of 1998, is the 930E. When the truck was initially released, it was rated as a 310-ton capacity hauler. Within a year, however, its payload rating was increased to 320 tons. But what made the 930E the talk of the industry was its use of an AC traction-drive system, developed jointly by Komatsu and GE. This type of diesel-electric drive had

been used extensively in the railroad locomotive industry, but this was the first time that an AC-drive system had been utilized in the design of a mining truck. The 930E has proven to be a very popular hauler in the mining industry, with well over 100 units delivered by late 1998.

One of the competing AC-drive systems to the Komatsu/GE package is built by Siemens for use in the 360-ton capacity Liebherr T-282. Liebherr Mining Equipment entered the large off-road hauler market in 1995 after purchasing Wiseda Ltd., of Baxter Springs, Kansas. During the truck's early design phase in 1996, it was referred to as the 320-ton capacity KL-2640. In 1997, the truck evolved into the 340-ton KL-2680, and in 1998, the designation was changed to the T-282, now rated as a 360-ton hauler. The T-282 is a diesel-electric drive truck, utilizing the Siemens/Liebherr AC traction wheel motor drive system. The truck is also designed around new 63-inch wheel rims, and the latest 55/80R63 size radial tires. Previously, the largest tire and wheel combinations utilized a 57-inch rim. But to get to payloads greater than 320 tons, a wider tire on a larger rim is needed to handle the load. The diameter of the new tires will stay the same as the 57-inch models, at about 12 feet. This size is the largest-diameter tire that can be economically transported over roadways because of underpass and lane width clearances. The prototype T-282 was unveiled in October 1998, at the Baxter Springs plant. The engine in the prototype truck is rated at only 2,750 gross hp for early field testing purposes, with the production trucks initially rated at 3,000 gross hp. This will increase as future higher-horsepower engines become available.

Liebherr Mining Equipment is also working on a new-concept truck called the TI-272, designed in cooperation with BHP of Australia. The prototype "proof of concept" truck, initially referred to as the ILMT (Innovative Large Mining Truck), and then as the IL-2600, began testing in May 1996. The test program's hauler carried a 240-ton payload, but the production trucks are rated as 300-ton units. The goal of this joint truck development between Liebherr and BHP was to reduce the total life cycle cost of a rear-dump mining truck by at least 15 percent. The weight of the hauler is reduced by eliminating the rear axle drive housing. In its place, the dump box acts as an integral part of the frame structure, working in parallel with the frame at all times. This allows

Caterpillar 789

Since its introduction in 1986, the Caterpillar 789 series of mining trucks has been the world leader in the 195-ton-capacity class of haulers. Power is supplied by a Caterpillar 3516 V-16 diesel engine, with a power rating of 1,800 gross hp and 1,705 fhp. The powertrain is mechanical—it utilizes a transmission and drive shaft, as opposed to the generator and wheel motor used in its diesel-electric driven counterpart. In 1992, Caterpillar released an upgraded model, the 789B. This was followed by the introduction of an even more refined 789C model in October 1998. The early Cat 789 pictured is working at the Rochelle North Antelope Complex, located south of Gillette, Wyoming. It is equipped with a high-volume coal body. Fully loaded, the 789 weighs in at 700,000 pounds. The Caterpillar 789B/C hauler's main rivals are the Komatsu 730E, the Unit Rig MT-3700B, and the Liebherr T-252. *ECO*

Caterpillar 793B

Announced in 1990, with the first trucks delivered into service in early 1991, the 240-ton-capacity Caterpillar 793 took the mining industry by storm. The basis of its success was its mechanical powertrain; no manufacturer before had ever designed a truck of this size that did not utilize diesel-electric drive. An upgraded version, the Caterpillar 793B, was introduced in October 1992. By the time Caterpillar replaced the 793B model with the new C series in mid-1996, more than 550 of the 793/793B haulers had been sold worldwide. The 793B is powered by a Caterpillar 3516 V-16 diesel engine, rated at 2,160 gross hp and 2,057 fhp, driven through a six-speed, electronically controlled, automatic power shift Cat transmission. The maximum loaded weight of the 793B is 830,000 pounds. *ECO*

the rear tires to be spaced evenly across the back of the truck, with widely spaced suspension struts on individual axle boxes, not unlike the design of the old VCON 3006 prototype. The rear wheel motors can be specified with either AC or DC systems, depending on the customer's requirements. In July 1997, after successful testing of the prototype IL-2600, BHP announced a license agreement with Liebherr to begin production of the 300-ton capacity truck program. At the time of this writing, Liebherr hopes to have the first T-272 units in the field sometime in 1999.

Being developed at the same time as Liebherr's T-282 truck is Caterpillar's massive 797 hauler. The Cat 797 is remaining true to its design heritage of utilizing a mechanical drive system, but this is no easy task. Rated with a 360-ton-maximum payload, the 797 utilizes the largest, most

advanced mechanical drivetrain ever conceived for use in a piece of Caterpillar earth-moving equipment. The massive Cat Diesel 3524B LS EUI, 24-cylinder engine was developed by connecting two Cat 3512B engines together at the crankshaft by means of a flexible coupling system. Power output is rated at a whopping 3,400 gross hp. This power is transferred to the rear drive differential through a computer-controlled, seven-speed automatic transmission—one of the most highly automated Caterpillar has ever designed, a

Caterpillar 793C

Caterpillar replaced its popular 793B hauler in June 1996 with the improved 793C. The Cat 793C is powered by the more efficient, cleaner-burning Cat 3516B EUI, V-16 diesel engine, rated at 2,300 gross hp and 2,166 fhp. The payload capacity remains unchanged at 240 tons. *ECO*

true engineering masterpiece. The Cat 797, like the Liebherr T-282, was designed from day one around 63-inch rims and tires. These are essential for the truck to reach its specified maximum payload capacity. In October 1998, the prototype 797 hauler was shipped down to Caterpillar's proving grounds in Arizona to start its long-term field testing program. A second unit followed in December 1998.

Not to be outdone by other mining truck manufacturers, Unit Rig, now a product division of Terex Mining, announced in late 1997 that it too was entering the ultra-hauler class with AC drive technology. The Unit Rig Lectra Haul MT-5500 (originally MT-4800) will utilize an AC wheel motor system, developed jointly by Unit Rig and the Power Conversion Systems Division of General Atomics. Engine choices of 2,800 and 2,700 gross hp will be initially offered. The MT-5500 will also ride on 63-inch rims and big 55/80R63 tires, the same as the Caterpillar and Liebherr ultra-haulers. The nominal payload capacity rating will be 340 tons. At the time of this writing, the prototype MT-5500 is tentatively scheduled to be ready in 1999.

Euclid-Hitachi Heavy Equipment is also in the design phase of a large-capacity Euclid hauler in the 340- to 360-ton payload class, designed around the Siemens AC-drive system. If all goes as planned engineering-wise, and if the market remains receptive, a prototype truck should be "in the iron" in the year 2000. The company incorporated the Siemens AC-drive technology in a specially built 280-plus-ton capacity Euclid R-280 in mid-1998 to see if the AC system is compatible with this hauler size class. The R-280 was shipped to a coal mine in eastern Pennsylvania for field evaluations testing in late 1998.

Very rarely seen in the North American mining industry are the BelAZ off-road haulers, built by the Byelorussian Automobile Plant; it's part of the BelAZ Trade Corporation (formerly BelavtoMAZ), headquartered in Minsk, in the Republic of Belarus, which was part of the old Soviet Union. The largest truck built by the company is its experimental ultra-hauler, the BelAZ 75501. Development started on the 75501 in 1988, with the first truck unveiled at the main Zhodino auto works plant in mid-1991. The massive truck looks like a cross between an articulated Euclid R-105 and the turbine Euclid R-210 on steroids. The BelAZ 75501 is a two-axle layout, with dual tires mounted at each corner and steering by means of an articulated chassis. Power is supplied by a Russian-built 12ChN1A 26/26 diesel locomotive engine, rated at 3,150 gross hp, which supplies power to the DC electric wheel motors. The payload capacity is 308 tons. About five percent of the truck's component systems were supplied by Komatsu, including the cab, hydraulics, and diagnostic systems. This was all right in 1991, but with Komatsu now in ownership of the Haulpak truck line, a different source of supply will have to be found for the production truck, which will be in the 340- to 360-ton range, if the local economy remains viable. As of 1998, the prototype 75501 has been working for the last few years in an open-cast coal mine in Nerungri, located in central Siberia.

Liebherr TI-272

The Liebherr TI-272 hauler is a joint engineering effort by Liebherr and Broken Hill Properties (BHP) of Australia. The "proof of concept," 240-ton-capacity prototype, originally referred to as the IL-2600, is known as the Innovative Large Mining Truck (ILMT). It was commissioned in May 1996 at the Saraji Coal Mine in Queensland, Australia, which is owned by Central Queensland Coal Association and operated by BHP Coal Pty., Ltd. The diesel-electric drive prototype pictured is powered by a MTU 16V-396 TE44 engine, rated at 2,500 gross hp. The loaded weight of the prototype is 765,000 pounds. The ILMT TI-272 concept truck is unique in that it does not have a rear axle housing connecting the rear frame together. Instead, the dump body acts as an integral part of the frame structure. This allows the rear tires to be spaced evenly across the back of the truck, with widely spaced struts on individual axle boxes. Production TI-272 haulers are capacity-rated at 300 tons. *Liebherr Mining Equipment*

Liebherr T-262

The 240-ton-capacity Liebherr T-262 actually got its start in life in 1982, as the Wiseda KL-2450 "King of the Lode" hauler—the mining industry's first true 220-ton-capacity, diesel-electric drive, two-axle production truck. By 1985, the capacity for the KL-2450 had increased to 240 tons. In 1995, Liebherr purchased the Wiseda firm and eventually changed the truck's designation in December 1997 to the T-262. Liebherr offers as many as seven engine configurations, with one of the more popular being the MTU 16V-396 TE44 diesel engine, rated at 2,500 gross hp. The standard loaded weight for the T-262 is 815,180 pounds, but specially prepared 250-ton payload trucks have been delivered in the past with loaded weights approaching 842,000 pounds. Pictured in November 1996, working at Peabody Coal's Lee Ranch Mine, near Grants, New Mexico, is a Liebherr T-262 (KL-2450) at the receiving end of a 56-cubic yard, 80-ton bucket of overburden. *ECO*

Liebherr T-282

Liebherr Mining Equipment officially unveiled its massive prototype T-282 "ultra" hauler in October 1998. Formerly known as the KL-2680 in its early design phase, the Liebherr T-282 is a 360-ton-capacity truck that utilizes a state-of-the-art Siemens/Liebherr AC traction-drive system. The new hauler is powered by a MTU/DDC 16V-4000 diesel engine rated at 3,000 gross hp, but the first prototype will be limited to 2,750 gross hp. The tires on the T-282 are huge 55/80R63 radials mounted on 63-inch rims. Fully loaded, the big Liebherr weighs in at 1,163,000 pounds. The length is 47 feet, 6 inches, with a 28-foot, 7-inch width. In late October, the prototype was shipped to its new home in the Powder River Basin at Thunder Basin Coal Company's Black Thunder Mine, near Wright, Wyoming. *Liebherr Mining Equipment*

2 BOTTOM DUMP HAULERS

n the world of the off-highway truck, the rear-dump haulers are the stars. But often overlooked are their close cousins, the bottom-dump haulers. Designed for hauling larger-volume, but lighter-weight material, the modern units of today can get quite large, especially those built for the coal industry. Development has often paralleled rear-dump engineering advancement, since many of these bottom-dump haulers utilize a tractor derived from a standard rear-dump chassis.

The earliest off-highway bottom dump specifically designed for that purpose from the ground up was built by Euclid Road Machinery in December 1933. This experimental tractor and trailer combination, referred to as the Euclid ZW, actually preceded the company's first off-highway rear-dump truck, the 1ZW, by a few months. Full production actually commenced on the 8-cubic yard, 10-ton-capacity Euclid 1ZW/42W bottom dump around March 1934. The tractor would share most of its components with the production 2ZW rear dump, the final version of the prototype 1ZW truck. In 1935, all of these models were referred to as Trac-Truk haulers. In September 1935, Euclid shipped its first off-highway coal hauler, the 1ZW/46W, to Truax-Traer Coal Company, located in Fiatt, Illinois. Three of these were built, all rated with 20-cubic yard, 17-ton capacities.

Not long after these Euclids went to work in Illinois, the Binkley Coal Company of Steelyville, Indiana, had four special coal haulers built for its Bobolink Mine, near Terre Haute. White Motor Co. supplied the specially prepared tandem-axle drive Model 691-SD-420 tractors, with Austin-Western building the single-axle bottom-dump trailers. The Austin-Western trailer could handle a payload capacity of 33 cubic yards, with a load limit of 25 to 30 tons. When these trucks went into service in late 1935 and early 1936, they were the largest known coal-hauling bottom dumps of the day.

Dart Trucks, which had been building trucks since 1903, entered the heavy-duty off-highway market in 1937. In 1939, the company built an experimental diesel-electric power coal train, consisting of a tandem-drive tractor and two 40-ton-capacity trailers. But with the war looming, the project had to be put on hold, while Dart's manufacturing facilities were converted to wartime needs.

Between 1936 and 1946, most of the available off-highway bottom-dump haulers were in the 25- to 32-ton payload class. But after World War II, with an expanding economy, more energy was needed to fuel America's burgeoning industries. To handle the larger amounts of coal produced in American mining operations, larger coal bottom-dump haulers were required. This would allow more manufacturers to break into the bottom dump market, since the larger volume of haulers needed now made the endeavor of designing and building these types of units more profitable.

During this time period, Euclid was the clear leader in the manufacture of tough, reliable, and profitable off-highway haulers,

Unit Rig Lectra Haul BD-270

The big 270-ton-capacity Unit Rig Lectra Haul BD-270 actually got its start as the BD-240. The first 240-ton coal haulers were shipped to the Caballo Mine south of Gillette, Wyoming, starting in December 1985. Not long after these first units went to work, additional haulers were ordered, specified at 270 tons capacity. After this, all of the mine's BD-240 haulers were upgraded to BD-270 specifications. The tractors of the BD-270 were initially based on the Mark 36 chassis. The engine was the Detroit Diesel 16V-149TIB, rated at 1,600 gross hp and 1,454 fhp. Today's models utilize the MT-3600B chassis. The length of the BD-270 is 96 feet, 9 inches, and it weighs 969,120 pounds fully loaded. In this picture, taken in October 1995, one of Caballo's BD-270 bottom dumps is being loaded by the mine's 70-cubic yard-coal loading shovel. *ECO*

both of the rear- and bottom-dump varieties. In 1947, the company introduced a very popular 40-ton-capacity coal hauler, the model 2TDT/94W. With its 40-ton payload capacity, it was a favorite choice in coal mining operations in the United States. This was followed by the 47-ton model 11TDT/124W in 1952.

Euclid's old adversary, Dart Trucks of Kansas City, Missouri, was not about to let this growing market for large coal bottom dumps be completely dominated by its arch rival from Cleveland, Ohio. In 1953, the company introduced a coal hauler that bested Euclid's latest entry by three tons—the Dart 50S-BDT. The Dart was rated as a 50-ton-capacity hauler, and it proved to be one very tough unit.

Euclid quickly countered this new threat from Dart by introducing its very popular 24TDT/128W coal hauler in 1954. Carrying a 51-ton payload, the "Euc" beat the Dart by one ton. However, its actual capacity in service may well have been less.

Many of the manufacturers of the day stretched the capacity and power ratings of their more competitive models to gain a marketing advantage.

While Euclid and Dart were battling for market share, LeTourneau-Westinghouse decided that now was a good time for it to introduce its own large-capacity coal hauler, the Haulpak LW-80. The LW-80 made its first appearance leading the Thanksgiving Day parade in its factory hometown of Peoria, Illinois, in 1957. In

Euclid CH-150
The 150-ton class of coal haulers was very popular throughout the industry in the 1970s and 1980s. Euclid's entry into the arena was the CH-150. The first pilot version was placed in 1977 at Peabody Coal Company's Universal Mine in Indiana. Power choices were either a Cummins or Detroit Diesel 12-cylinder engine, with power ratings of 1,050 gross hp and 1,000 fhp. The length of the complete unit was 79 feet, with a width of 17 feet, 5 inches. Fully loaded, the CH-150 weighed in at 505,600 pounds. *Euclid-Hitachi*

Terex 34-11C

Terex introduced its first 150-ton capacity coal hauler, the 34-11C, in late 1978. The tractor of the coal hauler utilized a modified chassis based on the 33-11C truck. Power was supplied by a GM Detroit Diesel 16V-92TA engine, rated at 880 gross hp and 840 fhp. The loaded weight of the entire unit was 480,000 pounds. The length of the coal hauler was 76 feet, 5 inches. The model was upgraded to the 160-ton capacity 34-12C/D in 1983. By 1986, Terex had stopped offering coal bottom-dump trailers in its product line. *ECO Collection*

December, it was delivered to Midland Electric, in Farmington, Illinois, to start its coal-hauling duties. The tractor on the LW-80 was based on the chassis of the revolutionary Haulpak LW-30 rear-dump truck. Payload was rated at 80 tons. In 1959, the designation on the coal hauler was changed to the "Model 80."

In 1958, Dart released a second model to add to its popular coal bottom-dump product line—the 70S-BDT. This 70-ton coal hauler was not as large as the Le-Tourneau-Westinghouse offering, but it was larger than anything Euclid had to offer at the time.

The 1960s belonged to bottom-dump haulers in the 100- to 120-ton class. Most of the major manufacturers introduced coal models in both of these size classes. Le-Tourneau-Westinghouse, now simply referred to as WABCO, released its 100-ton Model 100 Haulpak in 1962, followed by the 120-ton Model 120 in 1964. KW-Dart, formerly Dart Trucks, introduced its 100-ton

D4540 in 1962. This was followed by the release of the 120-ton D4651 in 1965.

Euclid came to the table with the 100-ton B-100 earth bottom dump in 1963, which proved to be one of the more popular large units for hauling dirt. In the coal hauler business, Euclid built a special fleet of CH-100 units equipped with 100-ton Darby bottom-dump trailers. Except for this special model, the Euclid Division of General Motors would not release another tractor/trailer coal hauler in the 1960s.

Just as Euclid was reducing its presence in the coal bottom-dump market, Mack Trucks was testing the water with its Model M-651XT-112BDT in 1965. The Mack coal hauler was pulled by a 635-gross-hp tractor based on the M-65X rear-dump chassis, pulling a 100-ton-capacity trailer. By 1970, the hauler was upgraded into the 110-ton Mack M-501XT-120BDT.

To help increase the productivity of the 120-ton coal haulers, Challenge-Cook Bros. of Industry, California, marketed a special

trailer option in 1968 called the C-CB Powerhorse-Coalhauler. This system consisted of a Challenge-Cook 318-gross-hp, two-axle power module, attached to one of its 75-ton bottom-dump coal trailers. This unit would then be connected to the rear end of the standard 120-ton tractor-trailer outfit. Two powered trailers could be used in conjunction with the main rig, totaling almost 300 tons of coal. These configurations proved to be a handful for operators when conditions were less than ideal, and only a few found a home in the industry.

After the oil crisis of the 1970s, there was a more concentrated effort to cut back on the import of outside energy supplies into the United States, and to further expand domestic fossil fuel production, such as coal. This spurred demand for, and led manufacturers of off-highway mining equipment to introduce, larger coal bottom-dump trailers in the 150-ton class. In 1975, Caterpillar released its 150-ton-capacity 776 Coal Hauler. Pulled by a 870-fhp tractor, based on the 777 hauler chassis, the 776 Coal Hauler would be the largest tractor/trailer bottom-dump outfit to be built and marketed by Caterpillar as a complete unit. Before this 150-ton unit, in 1974 Cat had introduced a 100-ton-772 Coal Hauler. In the 1960s, Caterpillar had offered through its dealerships the Athey 100-ton capacity PH660 coal trailer, and the PW660 earth bottom dump, to be utilized with the Cat Model 660 two-axle tractor. Athey, referred to as an allied manufacturer of optional equipment for Caterpillar, also produced all of the company's "rocker" rear-dump trailers.

In 1971, a new company by the name of Rimpull, located in Olathe, Kansas, started designing a new range of heavy-duty, bottom-dump tractor-trailers for the coal mining industry. Rimpull delivered its first mechanical-drive, 100-ton-capacity CW-100 coal hauler in 1973. By 1975, the company had introduced a 150-ton-capacity CW-150 model, pulled by a Rimpull-designed 1,050-gross-hp tractor. The company also entered the rear-dump hauler market in 1977. In late 1978, Rimpull introduced its largest mechanical-drive rear dump, the RD-120. Other models would follow, including those equipped as water trucks, identified as the "WT-Series."

After taking the wrong engineering road with its electric-drive truck program of the early 1970s, Dart made a commitment to the mechanical-drive powertrain and started to release all new designs of off-road haulers in the mid-1970s. Announced in 1974, the Dart Model 460 was the company's 150-ton coal bottom-dump hauler offering. In 1976, the designation for the hauler was changed to the 4150. In the early 1980s, the 4150 was upgraded into the 160-ton Dart 4160.

The largest bottom-dump hauler combination to be built by Dart was not for the coal industry, nor was it for hauling earth. Instead, it was for transporting salt. KW-Dart built and delivered its first two Model D4775 Salt-Trains to Exportadora de Sal, S.A., better known as ESSA, in Baja, California, in 1969. ESSA is the world's largest

Dart D5140

Some of the more unusual Dart bottom dumps are the D5140 Salt-Trains running at Exportadora de Sal, S.A., better known as ESSA, in Baja, California. ESSA is the world's largest producer of surface-mined salt. The Dart triple-trailer haulers are custom built for the extremely corrosive environment in which they operate. All exposed surfaces have special coatings and stainless steel fittings. The total capacity of the train is 420 tons, with each trailer capable of handling 140 tons. The total weight of a loaded hauler is 600 tons.

The Dart tractor is powered by a 12-cylinder, Detroit Diesel 12V-149T engine producing 1,050 gross hp. The D5140 can transport such a mammoth load with so little horsepower because the entire mining area is flat, and once the 200-foot-long Dart hauler gets going, there is little in the way of resistance. The first two KW-Dart D4775 units, the D5140's predecessors, were delivered in 1969. By the end of 1998, 13 Dart tractors and seven triple trailer sets had been supplied to ESSA. *ECO Collection*

producer of surface-mined salt, which is harvested from large solar evaporation ponds. These triple-trailer trains are custom built for the extremely corrosive environment in which they operate. All exposed surfaces have special coatings and stainless steel fittings. The total capacity of the train is 420 tons, which is 140 tons per trailer. Additional units have been added over the years, which are now pulled by Dart D5140 tractors. Today, seven trains are in operation—the seventh unit was delivered by Unit Rig at the end of 1994. New Dart tractors are ordered periodically to replace retired units. By the end of 1998, 13 Dart tractors had been supplied to ESSA to service the 7 triple-trailer sets.

The coal haulers of the 150-ton class were not necessarily the largest units produced in the 1970s, just the most popular. Coal mining operations were always looking for larger-capacity haulers, and a few manufacturers tried to step in with larger concept bottom dumps. One of these creations was the Euclid CH-220. The big "Euc" was a mechanical-drive, twin-powered, tandem-trailer coal hauler, with a combined hopper capacity of 220 tons. Power was supplied by two Detroit Diesel 16V-71T 16-cylinder engines, rated at 1,400 gross hp combined. One was located in the Euclid 207LDT tractor, and the other mounted at the rear of the first CH301 trailer. Only the tractor's rear axle

and the first hopper's rear axle were powered. The middle dolly and rear hopper were unpowered. The prototype CH-220 was delivered into service at the end of 1973 to a New Mexico coal surface mine, but operators soon found the CH-220 to have a few handling problems. The rear trailer had a tendency to wander about at speed and not track correctly behind the first hopper. Soon Euclid gave up on the whole concept of the CH-220; only one set was ever produced.

As the 1970s came to a close, Mack Trucks had been slowly losing interest in the manufacture of heavy-duty mining trucks. Mack made one final attempt at providing a bottom dump to the coal

Euclid CH-210
The Euclid CH-210 was a joint project between the Euclid division of VME and an Australian manufacturer. The tractor was a Euclid R-130 unit with either a Cummins or Detroit Diesel engine, rated at 1,350 gross hp and 1,200 fhp. The Australian company supplied the trailer, which had a 232-ton payload capacity. The maximum loaded weight of the coal hauler was 807,839.6 pounds. The length of the complete hauler was 84 feet, with a width of 20 feet. The first fleet of three trucks was delivered in December 1987 to BHP-Utah's Peak Dorons Mine in the Bowen Basin, Queensland, Australia. A total of 11 CH-210 haulers were eventually produced for BHP-Utah. The Australian supplier has since ceased production of the trailer unit. *Euclid-Hitachi*

Rimpull CWT-270

The Rimpull CWT-270 was one of the largest tandem coal bottom dumps ever produced for the coal mining industry. Powered by a 12-cylinder, Detroit Diesel 12V-149TI engine rated at 1,500 gross hp, the CWT-270 could handle a maximum 270-ton load of coal—150 tons in the first trailer and 120 tons in the rear unit. The combined capacity of both trailers was 353 cubic yards. The empty weight was 349,500 pounds, and the fully loaded weight was 889,500 pounds. The overall length was a long 149 feet, 8 inches. The only CWT-270 ever built was delivered in 1990 to Peabody Coal Company's Lynnville Mine in southern Indiana. But changes in the pit layout to accommodate the big tandem hauler's turning radius proved to be time consuming and not cost-effective. The CWT-270 was eventually converted into two separate coal haulers; the original 1,500-gross hp engine was replaced by a 1,200-gross hp unit in the tractor that pulled the lead 150-ton trailer. *Rimpull Corp.*

industry in the form of the 120-ton capacity M-50AXT-132BDT in 1977. But the company decided to focus on its over-the-road product line, and announced in 1979 that it was going to stop offering the M-series mining truck line. Some M-series haulers were still built in 1980 and 1981, but these were in response to production orders already in the works for a few of Mack's long-time customers.

For the most part, all of the larger-capacity bottom-dump haulers utilized a mechanical powertrain. But a diesel-electric-driven coal hauler was offered by Unit Rig in 1972—in the form of the 180-ton-capacity Lectra Haul BD-180. Pulled by a modified M-100 hauler chassis, the unit found some success in the marketplace. But mine owners were reluctant to add electric-drive haulers to operations that ran the more accepted mechanical-drive units. This was a shame, since the few fleets that were put into service performed quite well.

Unit Rig took another try at building an even larger diesel-electric drive coal hauler model in 1985, with its Lectra Haul BD-240. The BD-240, with its 240-ton capacity, was the largest single-trailer, coal bottom dump then available. The first units were

Unit Rig Lectra Haul BD-180

In February 1972, Unit Rig shipped its first diesel-electric drive, coal bottom dump, the Lectra Haul BD-180. The tractor unit on the BD-180 was based on the company's popular M-100 series hauler chassis, powered by a Detroit Diesel 12V-149TI engine, rated at 1,200 gross hp and 1,100 fhp. With a full 180-ton payload, the BD-180 weighed in at 596,200 pounds. The overall length of the hauler was 78 feet. *Terex*

Rimpull CW-180

Rimpull's newest design in large coal haulers is the 180-ton capacity CW-180. Most notable in its design is the placing of the radiator in the front of the tractor instead of on the upper deck, as in past Rimpull designs in this class. The CW-180 is powered by a Detroit Diesel 12V-149TI engine, rated at 1,350 gross hp. The standard rated capacity is 180 tons. The maximum trailer payload volume is 255 cubic yards heaped. The length of the CW-180 is 83 feet, 9 inches, and its fully loaded weight is 673,800 pounds. The first units of the CW-180 were delivered in 1996 to the BHP Navajo Mine, located near Farmington, New Mexico. *ECO*

delivered to the Caballo Mine near Gillette, Wyoming, in December 1985 and were an immediate success. Additional units were ordered, but this time they would be the even larger-capacity Lectra Haul BD-270 models. These 270-ton giants were just as well liked as the first 240-ton models. Soon, all of the original BD-240 hoppers were modified into 270-ton units.

Even though companies such as Caterpillar and Euclid no longer produced their own large-capacity bottom-dump trailers, they still supplied powerful prime movers to pull custom-made trailers built by an allied supplier. In 1987, an Australian manufacturer delivered three 232-ton-capacity trailers for use with modified Euclid R-130 tractors. These units were known as Euclid CH-210 coal haulers. In total, 11 sets were

eventually delivered to an Australian BHP-Utah coal mine. This same trailer manufacturer also built a fleet of 240-ton units, this time attached to 1,290-fhp Caterpillar 784B tractors in 1993, also destined for an Australian coal mining operation. But for one reason or another, the trailers were a bit on the expensive side, and the trailer company decided to suspend operations in the mid-1990s.

During the 1990s, large mining equipment manufacturers that fabricated their own large-capacity bottom-dump trailers continued to decline. Unit Rig was the exception, but not without some model casualties along the way. In April 1984, Unit Rig purchased the Dart product line from PACCAR in hopes of complementing its diesel-electric drive

offerings with mechanical-drive haulers and loaders. In July 1988, Unit Rig was purchased by Terex Corporation. After Unit Rig became a division of Terex Corp., little was done in the way of improving the Dart designs, with almost all of the engineering development geared toward the Lectra Haul trucks. Dart haulers were still sold, but in ever smaller numbers. By 1996, the Dart name was gone. All of the former models had been either discontinued or absorbed into the Unit Rig product line. The only Dart tractor/bottom dump still produced is the Model 5140. But this unit, the salt-hauler for ESSA, is a special order only and not a regular product offering.

The Lectra Haul BD-270 was the largest bottom-dump coal hauler in the world

MEGA Tandem CH100/Caterpillar 776B

Many outside firms, often referred to as allied companies, have arrangements with the original manufacturers of off-road equipment to supply specialized accessories to help meet the particular needs of a customer. One such company is MEGA Corp. of Albuquerque, New Mexico. MEGA specializes in supplying new or used equipment such as coal haulers, bottom-dump trailers, water wagons, and heavy transport trailers. Pictured is a set of MEGA's Magnum Tandem CH100 coal haulers, matched to a Caterpillar 776B tractor. The units are operating at the BHP La Plata Mine, north of Farmington, New Mexico. The total capacity of the tandem units is 200 tons. The 776B tractor is powered by a Cat D348, V-12 diesel engine, rated at 920 gross hp and 870 fhp. *MEGA Corp.*

when it was introduced in the late 1980s. But its reign would be cut short in 1990, when Rimpull would deliver two giant coal haulers. These were the mechanical-drive Rimpull CWT-270, and the CW-280. The CWT-270 was a tandem-trailer unit, pulled by a 1,500-gross hp, Rimpull-designed tractor based on Dart components. The first hopper carried a 150-ton payload, while the rear unit was rated with a 120-ton limit. The first CW-280 model was a single-trailer design, pulled by a modified Dart tractor equipped with a Caterpillar 1,500-gross hp diesel engine. With a 280-ton payload capacity, the hopper on the Rimpull was huge. At its maximum heaped capacity of 368 cubic yards, the CW-280 would have about 295 tons on board. But carrying this size of a load, day-in and day-out, would severely shorten the life-span of the entire

unit. The prototype unit, nicknamed "*Wilbur's Whopper*", was the first of two such haulers purchased by Peabody Coal for its Black Mesa mine in northern Arizona. Peabody would also eventually add another eight CW-280 coal haulers by the end of 1998 to its Kayenta Mine, which is right next door to the Black Mesa operation. All of these Rimpull trailers are pulled by modified Caterpillar 789 tractors.

As of 1999, one of the leading suppliers of off-highway bottom-dump coal haulers is MEGA Corp., located in Albuquerque, New Mexico. Mega is an original allied equipment supplier of trailers to Caterpillar, Komatsu, and Euclid. It also builds numerous models for modified, used tractors by various makes. Some of the company's largest units are its Magnum tandem-trailer combinations, built for high-speed, large-volume coal transport.

The first of these models, the Tandem CH100, was a dual-trailer outfit rated at 200 tons capacity. Five of these tandem-trailer sets were built for BHP's La Plata Mine near Farmington, New Mexico, and are all pulled by Caterpillar 776B tractors. The mine added two more trains in 1996, but this time they were the larger 240-ton-capacity Tandem CH120 trailers, pulled by Komatsu Haulpak 330M tractors. This Komatsu/Mega 240-ton combination proved so successful that another customer in Texas, North American Coal, specified the exact same configuration, receiving its first unit in late 1997.

In December 1993, Mega delivered the first of two CH260 coal haulers to Peabody Coal's Black Mesa Mine in Arizona. The tractor for the CH260 was a modified, used Caterpillar 789 hauler chassis, specially prepared by the local

Rimpull CW-280

The Rimpull CW-280 is currently the largest coal bottom-dump tractor/trailer combination the company has ever produced. The big Rimpull can easily handle a 280-ton-plus load in its large 368-cubic -yard heaped capacity trailer. The tractors for the first two CW-280 units were pulled by modified Dart units, powered by Caterpillar 3512 diesel engines rated at 1,500 gross hp. The empty weight of the CW-280 is 350,800 pounds; it weighs 910,800 pounds fully loaded. The length of the hauler is 91 feet, and it has a width of

21 feet. The first CW-280, nicknamed "Wilbur's Whopper", was delivered in 1990 to Peabody Coal's Black Mesa Mine in Kayenta, Arizona. As of 1998, all of the CW-280 coal haulers produced belong to Peabody. The company runs these large units at both its Black Mesa and Kayenta Mines, which are located next to each other. All of the CW-280 trailers at the Kayenta Mine are pulled by modified Caterpillar 789 tractors. *Urs Peyer*

Arizona Cat dealer, Empire Machinery Co. But this 260-ton coal hauler was just the appetizer. In July 1995, Mega delivered the first of three mammoth CH290 coal bottom-dump haulers to North American Coal's Coteau Properties Freedom Mine, near Beulah, North Dakota. The CH290, as of 1999, is the world's largest tractor/ trailer coal bottom-dump hauler. The trailer's massive hopper is rated at 290 tons, with a maximum rating of 302 tons and 407 cubic yards heaped. The three CH290 trailers are pulled by specially ordered Caterpillar 789B tractors. These were not used units, but new factory-produced 789B trucks with their dump bodies and associated hydraulic components deleted. Final design conversions were performed on-site by the local Bismarck Cat dealer, Butler Machinery Co. At almost 95 feet in length, it is four feet longer than the Rimpull CW-280.

Most of the really large bottom-dump haulers up until this point have been for the coal mining industry. Large earth-hauling types have been mainly limited to the 100- to 140-ton-capacity units. But in 1985, the Holland Loader Company from Billings, Montana, produced the first of two types of experimental, mechanical-drive, low-profile earth bottom dumps—to be utilized with its large belt loaders. One of these was the twin-engined Holland TE180. The TE180 was pulled by a two-axle tractor, powered by two Cummins diesel engines, with a combined rating of 1,200 gross hp. One engine was in the front tractor, and the other was at the rear of the 183-ton-capacity bottom-dump trailer. The other model was the Holland 180BD. The unit was in a tractor/trailer configuration, just like the previous unit, but the 180BD utilized a single 1,200-gross-hp Detroit Diesel engine up front. The capacity for this model was 200 tons.

MEGA Tandem CH120/Haulpak 330M

In 1996, the BHP La Plata Mine, located north of Farmington, New Mexico, added two additional MEGA Corp. tandem coal-hauling units to its fleet of tandem 200-ton-capacity trailers. Although usually pulled by Caterpillar tractors, these new MEGA Magnum Tandem CH120 trailers were matched to Komatsu Haulpak 330M, mechanical-drive tractors. Once loaded, this tandem hauler will make a 44-mile round trip, taking its 240-ton payload of coal to the San Juan Generating Station and then returning to the mine for another load. *ECO*

47

MEGA Tandem CH120/Haulpak 330M

These MEGA Magnum Tandem CH120 coal bottom-dump trailers are pictured here being pulled by a Komatsu Haulpak 330M tractor. The 330M is powered by a Komatsu 12V140Z-1 diesel engine, rated at 1,050 gross hp and 1,010 fhp. Before 1997, the 330M was equipped with a Cummins KTA38-C diesel, rated at 1,050 gross hp and 1,001 fhp. The entire vehicle, the tractor with its 240-ton-capacity trailers, is 125 feet in length. This yellow unit is working at North American Coal in Jourdanton, Texas, in December 1997. *KMS*

The Unitized Coal Haulers

In the 1970s, mining equipment manufacturers briefly fell in love with the concept of the unitized mining truck. A unitized hauler combines its drivetrain and bottom-dump hopper assembly on a single rigid frame, replacing the need for a separate tractor and trailer outfit. The unitized hauler saved on weight, had a better turning radius, and would not jackknife the way a tractor-pulled trailer might in certain working conditions.

The production unitized truck actually had its origins back in September 1952, when Ralph Kress, then with Dart Trucks, produced a concept sketch of a transit coal hauler that utilized two two-axle tractors, one at each end of a large bottom-dump hopper assembly. Kress joined Caterpillar in 1962, and by October 1965, his concept hauler finally became a reality, in the form of the mammoth 240-ton Caterpillar 786. The Model 786 was part of the Cat electric-drive truck program, which also included the models 779 and 783 haulers. The 786 was not a unitized hauler, but had some of the design and performance features that were similar to the benefits promised by one. The 786 had dual cabs, one at each end of the unit, so the unit could perform more like a shuttle-type coal hauler. Each of the 786's two tractors contained a complete Caterpillar-designed electric drive system, powered by a Cat D348 V-12 diesel engine driving the leading axle. The combined power output was 2,000 gross hp and 1,920 fhp. The first experimental prototype 786 went to work at the Southwestern Illinois Coal Corporation's Captain Mine in southern Illinois. In 1968, four additional 786 units were put into service at the mine. These units differed from the original prototypes in the placement of their engines, which were moved to the front of each tractor end instead of on top and behind the cabs like the original. But after Kress retired from Caterpillar in 1969, the electric-drive program was canceled. For liability reasons, all five of the 786 haulers had to be taken out of service at the Captain Mine. All were then parked in the mine's "boneyard" to be scavenged for parts when necessary.

Upon his retirement from Caterpillar, Kress joined his son's firm, Kress Corporation, located in Brimfield, Illinois. Under the guidance of the son, Ted Kress, the company had acquired a reputation for building well-engineered molten metal and slag pot carriers for the steel industry. Southwestern was pleased with the performance characteristics of the 786 coal hauler, and did not want to lose all of the engineering progress gained up until the time of the forced retirement of its five trucks. So Southwestern invited Ralph and Kress Corp. to continue where the 786 project left off. In May 1971, the company unveiled a newly designed coal hauler called the Kress CH-150 Coal Carrier. The CH-150 looked like a miniature Cat 786, with the same type of corrugated steel hopper side design utilized in both haulers. But the CH-150 was of a unitized construction utilizing a mechanical-drive system, with its 1,200-gross-hp diesel engine mounted in the rear of the unit, driving the rear wheels. The front end employed four steering wheels, with two mounted on each hydraulic-suspension steering strut. This design allowed the front wheels to be turned a full 90 degrees, giving the Kress the ability to make 180-degree turns and thus operate in very restricted pit layouts. Six CH-150 haulers were put into service at the Captain Mine, with many of these trucks running on wheels and tires that came off of the old retired Cat 786 units.

Goodbary Engineering Company of Cardin, Oklahoma, was the next firm to introduce a unitized truck to the mining industry, bringing out the Goodbary CP-2400 in 1975. Work started on the coal hauler in 1974, with the first unit delivered to Martiki Coal Corporation. Goodbary offered two models of the bottom dump, both utilizing diesel-electric drivetrains. The CP-2400-36 was a 1,000-gross hp, 130-ton coal hauler, while the CP-2400-40 was rated as

MEGA CH260/Caterpillar 789

MEGA Corporation's Magnum CH260 is the second-largest coal hauler the company has ever produced. The CH260 was designed to be matched with specially converted Caterpillar 789 trucks. These tractors first started life as used Cat 789 rear-dump haulers. They were modified by the local Cat dealer to take on the big 260-ton-capacity trailers. The 789 tractor is powered by a Cat 3516, V-16 diesel engine, producing 1,800 gross hp and 1,705 fhp. The complete unit is 91 feet, 6 inches long, and weighs in fully loaded at 951,240 pounds. The first tractor/trailer combination was delivered in December 1993 to Peabody Coal Company's Black Mesa Mine in Kayenta, Arizona. *MEGA Corp.*

a 1,600-gross hp, 170-ton unit. Differences in the Goodbary, as compared to the Kress hauler, were its front-mounted engine, diesel-electric drive, and single wheels at all four corners. Only four tires were used on the Goodbary. The hauler steered like a normal mining truck, and was not able to match the 90-degree steering capability of the Kress design. In 1980, the Goodbary hauler briefly became part of the Dart product line, marketed as the Dart 7000 series. In 1980, after William Seldon Davis left KENDAVIS Industries, the owners of Unit Rig, he bought the Cardin, Oklahoma, manufacturing facility that produced the old Goodbary for his new Wiseda operations. The unitized coal hauler truck concept would eventually be passed on to Wiseda, and marketed as the KL-2400. But the bad economic conditions of the time sealed the fate of the truck. In the end, no Goodbary-designed trucks were ever built under the Dart 7000/Wiseda KL-2400 names.

In 1974, Unit Rig announced its intention to build a unitized coal hauler much like the Kress design. The prototype model, the Lectra Haul BD-145 was a diesel-electric

continued on page 55

MEGA CH290/Caterpillar 789B
The first of three MEGA CH290 coal haulers arrived at the Freedom Mine near Bismarck, North Dakota, at the end of July 1995. The Caterpillar 789B tractors were powered by Cat 3516 diesel engines, rated at 1,800 gross hp and 1,705 fhp. The overall length of the unit is an impressive 94 feet, 8 inches. The CH290 is capable of transporting a maximum heaped payload in excess of 290 tons in its 407-cubic yard trailer. Fully loaded, the hauler weighs in at a hefty 1,027,840 pounds, or 514 tons. Pictured at Coteau Properties' Freedom Mine in October 1995, a new CH290 gets a walk-around inspection at its ready station just before heading off into the pit for a load of lignite coal. *ECO*

MEGA CH290/Caterpillar 789B
When it comes to big coal haulers, the giant MEGA CH290 ranks as one of the largest tractor/trailer combinations of all time. The MEGA-designed Magnum trailer was so large, in fact, that it could not be built at MEGA's facility in Albuquerque, New Mexico. Instead, the final assembly work was subcontracted to WOTCO in Casper, Wyoming. The massive 290-ton-plus load is handled by a Caterpillar 789B tractor, ordered new from the factory, without its dump body and associated hydraulic system. The final conversion of the 789B chassis was handled by the local Cat dealer in Bismarck, North Dakota. The CH290 was specially ordered by Coteau Properties Company, a subsidiary of North American Coal Corporation, for use at its Freedom Mine, located near Bismarck. *ECO*

Goodbary CP-2400/36

Goodbary Engineering Company introduced its first diesel-electric-drive CP-2400/36 bottom-dump coal hauler in 1975, delivering the first unit to Martiki Coal Corporation. The first Goodbary CP-2400/36 (CP stands for Coal-Porter) was powered by a 12-cylinder Caterpillar D348 diesel engine, rated at 1,000 gross hp and 990 fhp. Fully loaded, the hauler weighed in at 400,000 pounds with a maximum 130-ton payload rating. A second 170-ton-capacity model, the CP-2400/40, was also offered. Pictured working at the Caballo Mine south of Gillette, Wyoming, in October 1995, a CP-2400/36 is being loaded with 130 tons of coal. By mid-1996, the mine had retired the last of its Goodbary haulers. *ECO*

WABCO 170 Coalpak

In the last half of the 1970s, a new breed of bottom-dump, unitized haulers, targeted exclusively at the coal market, began to appear. WABCO's entry into this field was the 170 Coalpak. The diesel-electric-drive 170 Coalpak was first announced by WABCO in 1977, with the first unit produced in February 1979. The coal hauler carried its Detroit Diesel 16V-149TI engine in the rear for better traction. The power ratings for this unit were 1,600 gross hp and 1,450 fhp. The maximum capacity was 170 tons in its 246-cubic yard body. Fully loaded, the Coalpak weighed in at 573,000 pounds with an overall length of 56 feet, 6 inches. A fleet of these trucks was put into service at Kerr-McGee's Jacobs Ranch Mine in Wright, Wyoming, in 1979. They were in active service until 1996, when the fleet was retired and sold off. *KMS*

Caterpillar 786

In October 1965, Caterpillar introduced a massive, 240-ton-capacity prototype bottom-dump coal hauler, designated the 786. At the time, it was the largest type of hauler ever constructed by any manufacturer. The Cat 786 was in the same family of electric-drive-haulers as the 779 and 783. The same Cat D348, V-12 diesel engine was used in all of these trucks, but the 786 had two engines, one at each end, driving the leading axles through a Caterpillar-designed electric-drive system. The power ratings were 2,000 gross hp and 1,920 fhp. Pictured is the upgraded version of the Cat 786 from 1968. Only four Cat 786 coal haulers were built in this configuration—the pilot version had the engines mounted on top of the tractors, not in front. All five units worked at the Southwestern Illinois Coal Corporation's Captain Mine (now owned by Arch Minerals) in southern Illinois. The 786 was 96 feet in length, and weighed in fully loaded at 670,000 pounds. After 1969, all work on the electric-drive hauler programs by Caterpillar ended. These incredible haulers were soon relegated to the Captain Mine's bone-yard, and scrapped by the mid-1980s. *ECO Collection*

Kress CH-300

One of the most unusual trucks working in the mining industry today is the Kress CH-300 bottom-dump coal carrier. This incredible unit, unofficially nicknamed the "Pit-Bull," has a rated capacity of 300 tons in its 444-cubic yard coal body. The length of the CH-300 is 67 feet, 9 inches, and its width is 22 feet, 9 inches. Unique to this type of hauler is its ability to turn its dual front steering wheels at 90-degree angles, enabling the mammoth hauler to turn in less than 73 feet, just a little over its overall length. *Kress Corp.*

Continued from page 51

drive, 1,200-gross-hp, 145-ton coal hauler. The BD-145 had its engine mounted in the rear of the unit, and had a steering system similar to the Kress hauler, which allowed the BD-145 to make full 90-degree turns with the front, dual-tire wheel assemblies. After testing of the single prototype at the Captain Mine in 1977, design changes were made on the hopper construction and the front end. In October 1978, the coal hauler was officially released as the Lectra Haul BD-30. The eight-tire unit's payload was now rated at 160 tons, but most major design parameters remained unchanged. But the BD-30 just couldn't find a customer base, and only a few were ever built.

The last company to market a Kresslike hauler was WABCO, with its 170 Coalpak. WABCO first announced the Coalpak concept in 1977, with the first unit built in February 1979. The hauler had its 1,600-gross-hp diesel-electric drivetrain mounted in the rear like the Kress, but utilized a more conventional steering system and was not capable of 90-degree turns. The payload capacity was 170 tons. Like all of the unitized coal haulers before it, except the original Kress Coal Carrier, the Coalpak fell victim to the hard economic times of the day.

The unitized coal carrier built by Kress survived its attacks from the competition because it had faster travel speeds than the slower electric-drive models, and a better payload-to-weight ratio. As of 1998, the largest models offered by Kress are its CH-186, CH-200, and the monstrous CH-300.

The CH-300 is the largest coal carrier ever built by the company. The big unit is powered by a rear-mounted 1,800-gross-hp Caterpillar 3516 diesel engine and transmission, which drives the rear wheels. The capacity of the bottom-dump hopper is 300 tons and 444 cubic yards heaped. The CH-300 was specially built for North American Coal's Coteau Properties, for hauling lignite at its Freedom Mine, which is also the home for the Mega/Cat CH290 coal haulers. The first hauler was delivered to the mine in late 1993, followed by two more units shortly thereafter. As of 1999, Coteau (French-Canadian for rolling hills) has the distinction of owning and operating the world's largest tractor-pulled bottom-dump coal haulers and unitized bottom-dump coal carriers.

Kress CH-300

The first units produced of the 300-ton-capacity, mechanical-drive Kress CH-300 were equipped with Caterpillar's 3516 diesel engines, producing 1,800 gross hp. The entire drivetrain is located in the rear of the unit, driving the rear wheels. The empty weight of the hauler is 290,000 pounds with a maximum loaded weight of 890,000 pounds. The first fleet of three haulers was put into service by late 1993, at Coteau Properties' Freedom Mine in North Dakota. *ECO*

3 MODERN LOADING EXCAVATORS

To load the massive mining haulers that are at work today throughout the world, you need an equally large loading shovel or excavator. These brutes are divided into two major classes of machines—cable shovels and hydraulic excavators. The hydraulic category of machines is then divided into two types—the front shovel and the backhoe or mass excavator. Large cable excavators are available as shovels only. In years past, backhoe cable excavators were very common, but they were never produced in sizes that could be considered large mining machines.

During the last few years, the manufacturers that build these massive excavators, some with well over 100 years of experience in building earth-moving equipment, have gone through some significant changes. In some ways, the industry is contracting as a whole. Instead of numerous companies offering select product lines, large corporate conglomerates now sell complete packages of equipment. In many cases, today's mining equipment customers can get the trucks, loaders, and shovels they need from a single source. This way, the manufacturers can often offer complete package deals that include long-term service contracts, leasing arrangements, parts and warranty extensions, machine backups, and, quite often, a better price. Companies that offer only a limited product line can often find themselves at a disadvantage when bidding a contract.

For decades, the world's top three cable mining shovel manufacturers have been Bucyrus-Erie of South Milwaukee, Wisconsin; Marion Power Shovel of Marion, Ohio; and P&H Harnischfeger of Milwaukee, Wisconsin, which is located just across town from the Bucyrus facilities. But in the last few years, the two oldest firms, Bucyrus-Erie and Marion, have weathered profound changes.

The Bucyrus-Erie Company, which has a company history stretching back to 1880, announced in early 1996 that it was changing its name to Bucyrus International to better reflect the company's position in the global market. The Erie name had become part of the company's title after the Bucyrus Foundry & Manufacturing Co. merged with the Erie Steam Shovel Co. in 1927. In April 1997, Bucyrus International signed a letter of intent to purchase the Marion Power Shovel Company outright. By September, Marion's 113 years of existence quietly came to an end. Founded in 1884 as the Marion Steam Shovel Co., it was always one of Bucyrus' closest rivals. Now there is only Bucyrus International and Harnischfeger. Many will mourn the passing of Marion, but it seems only proper that it was Bucyrus that eventually wound up with the company.

In Marion's last few years of production, it released one of its largest mining shovels—the 351-M series. The 351-M was essentially an improved and upgraded version of the 301-M series of electric mining shovels, of which 14 were built and placed in service—four in Australia, two in Siberia, five in Canada, and three in the United States. Marion built and sold three 351-M shovels between 1995 and 1996, with the last one delivered to Fording River Coal, near Elkford, British Columbia, in July 1996. Marion had also marketed a 251-M model in 1996 as a replacement for its popular 201-M series, but none were ever sold. The last two machines to be built and delivered by Marion after the last 351-M were older, smaller model 182-M shovels, both destined for India. After this, no more machines were sold carrying the Marion name.

P&H 4100

Since its introduction in 1991, the P&H 4100 series has gained a worldwide reputation as a tenacious, hard-rock digging machine. Working at Powder River Coal Company's Caballo Mine in Gillette, Wyoming, this 59-cubic yard capacity 4100 is loading a 260-ton capacity Unit Rig Lectra Haul MT-4400. This shovel went into service in February 1995 and was the second such machine on site. The Caballo Mine is also home to the first 4100 prototype unit. The average working weight of the P&H 4100 is 1,225 tons. *ECO*

Marion 351-M ST
The impressive 85-ton capacity Marion 351-M series was an upgrade to its popular 301-M shovel line. The first unit went to work at Suncor's tar sand operations, just north of Fort McMurray, in northern Alberta. The 56-cubic, yard shovel was officially handed over to Suncor on October 30, 1995. The overall working weight of this 351-M ST is 1,300 tons. *ECO Collection*

Marion 351-M HR
The third and last of the Marion-built 351-M shovels to go into service went to Fording River Coal, located near Elkford, British Columbia, Canada. It was officially handed over to the mine on July 29, 1996. Fording's big 351-M HR is equipped with a 56-cubic yard dipper, rated at 85 tons capacity. The biggest visual difference between this 351-M and the other two units, besides its color, is that its operator's cab is mounted on the right side of the machine housing. Suncor's 351-M has it mounted on the left, and Black Thunder's has dual cabs. The weight of the 351-M HR is 1,253 tons. *ECO*

After Bucyrus International officially became the owner of Marion Power Shovel in September 1997, plans were immediately put into effect to close the old Marion facilities in Marion, Ohio, and integrate the company's operations into Bucyrus' South Milwaukee offices and plants. Marion's largest shovel offering would now be identified as the Bucyrus 351-M, while key models of the 8000 series draglines would be marketed as Bucyrus products. But Marion's old mining drills, along with the Marion name and trademark, were now history. The current 351-M model joins the rest of Bucyrus' product line of electric mining shovels which also includes the 495-BI series. Both the 351-M and the 495-BI are 85-cubic yard capacity machines, but because of differing features, each has its own particular niche in the marketplace. It will take a few years before many of the Marion designs can be fully integrated into Bucyrus' existing product offerings. In early 1999, the first Bucyrus 351-M shovel was put into service at Suncor's oil sand operations in northern Alberta. This is also the home of the first Marion 351-M shovel built, which went on line in October 1995. Suncor liked the first 56-cubic yard 351-M so much, it wanted another one just like it. But this time, it will have the Bucyrus name displayed high on the boom.

Across town from Bucyrus are the offices and manufacturing plants of P&H Mining Equipment, part of Harnischfeger Industries. For the past decade, P&H has been one of the world leaders in the production of electric mining shovels. They have built some of the finest, longest lasting, and most reliable cable shovels ever offered to the mining industry.

P&H was founded in the same year as Marion, in 1884, as Pawling & Harnischfeger, Engineers and Machinists. Thirty years would elapse before the company would introduce its first excavator—the P&H Model 210. Later, in 1933, it released its first electric mining shovel, the 2-cubic yard Model 1200WL. Another major milestone in the history of the company's shovels occurred in 1969, when P&H put its first 2800 series mining shovel to work. This shovel was the first to feature the company's exclusive Electrotorque system for converting AC to DC power. It was still in service as of 1998, working at Elkview Coal in Sparwood, British Columbia. The first of four 25-cubic yard units to be shipped, this unit carried the mine's shovel equipment number 313 (formerly 309), and now has sustained well over 131,000 hours of operation—an incredible number for a large shovel in the mining industry. The 2800 series is still in production, with the latest version, the 2800XPB, a class leader in the 46-cubic yard capacity range.

The company's largest and most popular offering as of 1999 is its incredible 4100 series, introduced in July 1991. Weighing in at an average of 1,335 tons with standard bucket capacities ranging from 56 to 60 cubic yards, the 4100/4100A shovel models are the "top dogs" in the 85-ton capacity class, with more than 80 sold by the end of 1998.

Though all of the P&H 2800 and 4100 shovels are stellar performers, there are a few that stand out from the rest in terms of capacity—these are the coal loading shovels. Largest of this group is the long-range 4100A LR, delivered in 1995 and now working at the Rochelle North Antelope Complex in the Powder River Basin (PRB) of Wyoming. With its 80-cubic yard bucket, it is second only to Black Thunder's 84-cubic yard Marion 351-M LR, which is the world's largest-capacity two-crawler coal loading shovel. Other big P&H models include two field-modified shovels, both in the PRB. One is an older 2800XP working at the Caballo Mine, retrofitted with a 70-cubic yard coal bucket. The other is the original 2800XPA model at the Rochelle North Antelope Complex, which was first delivered in June 1988. In 1998 it was converted into a long-range, 64-cubic yard coal loading shovel.

In addition to the coal loading shovels, the special "tar sands" units, built for operating in the harsh conditions found in the oil

Marion 351-M LR

The second Marion 351-M to be put into service was a special dual-cab, coal loading shovel version for Thunder Basin Coal Company's Black Thunder Mine, located in the Powder River Basin near Wright, Wyoming. The 351-M LR carried a longer boom of 75 feet, compared to the standard unit's boom length of 60 feet. Dipper size is a massive 84 cubic yards of coal and is rated at 63 tons payload. Approximate overall weight of the long-range version is 1,335 tons. The big shovel started operations at the mine in June 1996. *ECO* sand operations of northern Alberta, also merit special attention. The 4100TS is equipped with a standard 58-cubic yard capacity dipper, and because of its special weight-saving design, it can handle a 100-ton payload. The 4100TS is also equipped with the largest crawler pads ever designed for a loading shovel, measuring 11 feet, 6 inches wide per side. Overall working weight of these special units is 1,488 tons. The first 4100TS began working at Suncor Energy's mining operations in October 1998. This was followed by two more units in early 1999, which were shipped to Syncrude's oil sand operations adjacent to Suncor's property boundaries.

The largest two-crawler mining shovels ever produced by any company are the massive P&H-5700 series machines, introduced in May 1978. Only five 5700 shovels have ever been manufactured. The third one, built in 1987, was not designed as a mining shovel but as a barge-mounted dredge. Built for Great Lakes Dredge & Dock Company, the *Chicago,* as it was named, could be equipped with a shovel front or a clamshell attachment. But the life of the *Chicago* would not have a happy ending. On October 5, 1996, while the barge was being moved to a new working location off the coast of Denmark, the *Chicago* was swamped by high waves, 60 miles from the Esbjerg Port. It then capsized and sank to the bottom of the North Sea. The other four land-loving 5700 mining shovels are all still on active duty, with one in the United States and the other three in Australia. The model line is technically discontinued, but if a customer really wanted one, P&H would be more than happy to build it for them.

In the last decade, large hydraulic excavators have slowly chipped away at the cable shovel's dominance in the mining industry. For shorter-term operations, the hydraulic front shovel is a very popular choice. Its ability to selectively dig in certain

Bucyrus 495-BI

Bucyrus International's largest mining shovel designed in-house, as of 1999, is its 495-BI series, introduced in mid-1996. Pictured working in a copper mine in Chile, this Bucyrus 495-BI is loading a 255-ton capacity Komatsu 830E Haulpak truck. This shovel, owned by Collahuasi, is equipped with a 56-cubic yard bucket, rated at 85 tons capacity. The length of the boom is 64 feet, with an overall working weight of 1,228 tons. By the end of 1998, over 30 of the 495-B series mining shovels had been sold worldwide. *ECO Collection*

working areas, plus its greater site-to-site mobility are legitimate selling points for the large hydraulic machines. The one big drawback is machine life. The typical life span of a hydraulic unit is around 60,000 hours of service. Large cable shovels often exceed 100,000 hours and often outlive the mining operation for which they were built.

The principal manufacturers of large hydraulic excavators have also been going through some major changes of late, with most forming some type of an alliance with an associated equipment provider. Nowhere is this more evident than with the European manufacturers of these machines—Demag, O&K, and Liebherr.

Mannesmann Demag, the company that in 1954 introduced the world's first fully hydraulic excavator, signed an agreement in November 1995 to form a 50-50 joint venture company with Komatsu, Ltd. The new entity would produce hydraulic excavators under the name Demag-Komatsu GmbH. In February 1999, Komatsu agreed to purchase 100 percent ownership of the joint venture, which is now called Komatsu Mining Germany GmbH. As of 1998, the three largest models marketed by the company are the H655S, the H455S, and the H285S. The biggest of these is the H655S, which is rated as a 46-cubic yard front shovel. The H655S replaced the former H485SP model

P&H 2800XPB

The Harnischfeger P&H 2800 series of electric shovels have been stellar performers in mining operations around the world since first going into service in 1969. Pictured working at ASARCO's Mission Mine, near Sahuarita, Arizona, is the latest example of this popular P&H shovel, the 2800XPB. Delivered in June 1995, this unit is equipped with a 46-cubic yard dipper with a 58-foot boom. The average working weight of the 2800XPB shovel is 1,121 tons. *ECO*

P&H 4100A

Pictured working at the ASARCO Mission Mine, near Sahuarita, Arizona, is the 50th P&H 4100-series shovel sold. Delivered in July 1996, this 60-cubic yard, 85-ton capacity 4100A shovel can load the mine's 240-ton capacity Haulpak 830E haulers in three very quick passes. The working weight of the current P&H 4100A shovels is 1,336 tons. By the end of 1998, more than 80 of the 4100 series machines had been sold around the world. *ECO*

which was the most powerful of the H485 series. The H485, which dates back to 1986, was the world's largest hydraulic excavator in its day.

The first of the H655S front shovels was shipped during the winter months of early 1998, over the frozen ice bridges of the Canadian Northwest Territories to the newly opened BHP Ekati Diamond Mine. It was critical that the shovel be delivered on time; during the spring thaw, the ice bridges melt, and there is no way in or out of the mine except by plane. In May 1998, the big Komatsu Demag H655S was ready to take its first bucketful. A special version of the Komatsu Demag H655S was put into service in January 1999 called the H740 OS. Built for Klemke Mining Corp., it is designed to work in the extremely tough digging conditions found in the oil sand mining operations located just north of Fort McMurray, in Alberta. Unique to this model is its wider car body and track pads for greater stability while loading, three swing transmissions, and parallel linkage. The power is supplied by two Caterpillar 3516B diesel engines, producing 4,400 gross hp. Bucket capacity is 52.3 yards. The overall working weight of the H740 OS is 815 tons. Klemke is also the owner of the first Demag H685SP front shovel, which is actually a H485SP model. After the H685SP had been delivered, Demag decided to change the models designation to H485SP. Same machines, just different nomenclature.

Another German company, O&K Orenstein & Koppel Aktiengesellschaft, whose history dates back to 1876, has recently undergone major corporate changes as well. In December 1997, the firm announced that it was going to sell its large mining hydraulic excavator company, O&K Mining GmbH, to Terex Corporation. In early 1998, the deal was finalized; O&K Mining joined a newly formed company division called Terex Mining Group, headquartered in Tulsa, Oklahoma. It will be responsible for all marketing of O&K mining excavators and Unit Rig mining haulers. To give the new division a complete integrated look, all of the O&K and Unit Rig products are now painted white with red trim and markings. The three largest of the O&K excavators to join the Terex company are the RH400, the RH200, and the RH170. Since its introduction in 1995, the 27.5-cubic yard RH170 has carved out a sizable chunk of machine sales in its capacity class. The RH200 is the best-selling large hydraulic excavator among machines weighing 500 tons or more. And the incredible RH400 is simply the largest-production hydraulic excavator of the 20th century.

The massive O&K RH400 was codeveloped by O&K and Syncrude Canada, Ltd., for use in its oil sand operations in northern Alberta. After 18 months of intensive design work, in early August 1997, the first RH400 left the O&K Dortmund factory in Germany; it arrived in Fort McMurray, Alberta, in mid-September. The RH400 was officially launched at Syncrude's new North Mine site on October 22, 1997. After a few early operating problems were ironed out, Syncrude's "final acceptance test" was carried out on the giant front shovel in December, and it passed with flying colors. In May 1998, a second RH400 unit joined the first machine at the North Mine. Weighing in at 910 tons, with a bucket capacity of 55 cubic yards, the RH400 is starting to tread in markets that have been dominated by large cable shovels. Other larger hydraulic machines will undoubtedly enter the market in the years to come, but as of 1999, the RH400 is king of the hydraulic front shovels.

As part of a similar effort to offer a more comprehensive product line, in 1995 Switzerland-based Liebherr purchased Wiseda, Ltd., a very highly respected manufacturer of large mining haulers. This made it possible for Liebherr to offer its customers perfectly matched hauler and shovel combinations from one source. The large mining excavators and haul trucks are marketed in North America by Liebherr Mining Equipment Co.

All of Liebherr's big hydraulic excavators are built at its facilities in Colmar, France. The three largest Liebherr excavators are the R994, R995, and R996. As of 1999, the R996 is Liebherr's current heavy hitter. Though not in the same operating class as the giant O&K RH400, the R996 is still a massive earth-moving machine. Introduced in May 1995, the big Liebherr is

continued on page 68

O&K RH200

Since its introduction in 1989 through the end of 1998, more than 63 O&K RH200 excavators have been sold worldwide, making it the best-selling large hydraulic mining excavator above 500 tons. The RH200 is powered by two Cummins KTA38C-1200 diesel engines, rated at 2,400 gross hp and 2,102 fhp combined. The standard bucket capacity is 33 cubic yards, with an average overall working weight of 529 tons. Shown working in September 1996 at Barrick Goldstrike's gold mining operation near Elko, Nevada, is the second RH200 to be sold in the United States—the 46th overall. *ECO*

O&K RH400

When it comes to big front shovels, they all take a back seat to the massive O&K RH400, the world's largest hydraulic excavator as of 1998. Designed by O&K with the input and assistance of Syncrude engineers, the first unit went to work in the oil tar sands of the new Syncrude North Mine north of Fort McMurray, Alberta, in October 1997. The first RH400 was powered by a pair of Cummins K2000E diesel engines, rated at 4,000 gross hp and 3,350 fhp. A second RH400 shovel joined the first unit in May 1998, but this time with more power dialed in, and now rated at a healthy 3,650 fhp. By the end of 1998, Cummins' new Quantum QSK60 diesel engines were installed in the first RH400 shovel, replacing the temporary K2000E units. These engines increased power output to a whopping 5,000 gross hp and 4,000 fhp. These new diesels can easily produce more than their rated 4,000 fhp, but this type of arrangement increases the life and reliability of the powerplants. *ECO*

P&H 5700XPA

Harnischfeger delivered its last massive P&H 5700-series shovel to Coal and Allied Industries' Hunter Valley Mine in July 1991. This shovel and its sister machine at R. W. Miller & Company Proprietary Limited's Mount Thorley Mine in Queensland, Australia, are both 5700XPA models. Both shovels are equipped with 57.5-cubic yard dippers and have operating weights of 2,100 tons each. These units are still the largest two-crawler loading shovels in existence today. Only five P&H 5700 series machines were built, with the third being mounted on a barge as a dredging shovel or clam. *Harnischfeger*

O&K RH400

The O&K RH400 weighs in at a stout 910 tons, more than 155 tons heavier than the former record holder, the Komatsu Demag H485SP. The bucket on the RH400 is rated at 55 cubic yards with an 80-ton payload capacity, and is specially designed to dig in very abrasive oil sands. The height to the top of the operator's cab is 29 feet, 9 inches. The crawlers are 32 feet, 8 inches in length, and 6 feet, 7 inches in width. *ECO*

Komatsu Demag H455S

The large Komatsu Demag H455S has been in a two-fisted battle for market share with its main nemesis, the O&K RH200, since it was introduced in mid-1995. Both machines are classified as 33-cubic yard shovels. The H455S is powered by two Cummins KTTA38-C diesel engines, rated at 2,250 gross hp and 2,144 fhp, with an overall working weight of 540 tons. Pictured working at Suncor's oil sands mining operations north of Fort McMurray, Alberta, is the first H455S delivered into service in North America. This is the same H455S that was on display at the September 1996 MINExpo in Las Vegas, Nevada. *ECO*

Demag H685SP

Shown working at Syncrude in October 1997 is the only Demag H685SP front shovel belonging to Klemke Mining Corporation, a major mining subcontractor to the large oil sand producers. The big Demag is powered by a pair of Caterpillar 3516DI-TA diesel engines, producing 4,000 gross hp and 3,730 fhp. The bucket size is 46 cubic yards, with a 70-ton capacity rating.

The overall working weight is 755 tons. After the H685SP was commissioned in March 1995, the designation for the model was changed to the H485SP series. It is the same machine with the same specifications, just different nomenclature. *ECO*

Komatsu Demag H655S

In May 1998, Komatsu Demag put its first H655S hydraulic front shovel to work at BHP's Ekati Diamond Mine in the Northwest Territories. This new series is the replacement for the previous H485S/SP models. Key to the H655S is its redesigned shovel front end including the boom, stick, and bucket, and its larger and more powerful hydraulic cylinders. The shovel gets its power from two Caterpillar 3516DI-TA diesel engines, rated at 3,728 gross hp and 3,714 fhp. The bucket size is the same as the previous H485SP model, 46 cubic yards with a 70-ton capacity. The working weight is also the same at 755 tons. As the picture clearly illustrates, the Komatsu Demag H655S sports a very large bucket indeed! *KMS*

Liebherr R996 Litronic
Since its introduction in May 1995, the Liebherr R996 Litronic has proven to be a very durable mining excavator. The R996 gets its power from two Cummins K1800E diesel engines with outputs of 3,600 gross hp and 3,000 fhp combined. The largest front shovel bucket offered by Liebherr is rated at 44.4-cubic yards capacity. The average working weight of the R996 is 633 tons. *Liebherr-France*

Continued from page65

proving itself in the toughest digging conditions—especially in Australia, where the R996 is a favorite, either in front shovel or backhoe configurations.

Though not as formidable as the R996, the Liebherr R995 still has the muscle to get the job done. In September 1998, Liebherr delivered its first P995 excavator, configured as a barge-mounted, backhoe dredge. The second unit, equipped as a backhoe, was put in service at a coal mining operation in Spain in November 1998. Configured as a front shovel, the R995 weighs in at 433 tons, and is equipped with a standard 30-cubic yard bucket.

In December 1993, VME Industries North America and Hitachi Construction Machinery Company, Ltd., of Japan launched a new joint venture company, formed from Euclid's U.S. operations and called Euclid-Hitachi Heavy Equipment, Inc. This subsidiary company, currently jointly owned by Volvo (20 percent) and Hitachi (80 percent), was one of the first to combine and market two separate corporate mining hauler and excavator product lines from a single source. Hitachi's top hydraulic mining excavators are the EX2500, the EX3500-3, and the EX5500. The largest of these, the EX5500, was officially introduced in July 1998 at the Syncrude Aurora Mine, when the machine was handed over to its new owners, North American Construction. Weighing in at 570 tons, with a 35.5-cubic yard bucket, the EX5500 front shovel is in the same league as the Komatsu Demag H455S and the class-leading O&K RH200.

The big Hitachi joins many of the world's largest hydraulic excavators working in the Athabasca Oil Sands Deposit of northern Alberta, canals which is approximately twice the size of Lake Ontario. The Athabasca and Alberta's three other oil sand deposits contain almost five times more oil than the conventional oil reserves of Saudi Arabia. But the oil is locked in a mixture of sand, bitumen, mineral-rich-clays and water. Because of

Caterpillar 5230
The Caterpillar 5230 is the largest hydraulic excavator built by the company as of 1998. On the mining scene since 1994, the 5230 has been a standout performer, ideally suited to load trucks in the 150- to 200-ton capacity class. The 5230 front shovel (FS) carries a 22.2-cubic yard bucket, while its backhoe mass excavator (ME) counterpart utilizes a 21-cubic yard general purpose bucket and a 36-cubic yard bucket for coal. Power is supplied by a Cat 3516 EUI diesel engine, rated at 1,575 gross hp and 1,470 fhp. The working weight of the 5230 FS is 351 tons. *Caterpillar*

the large volumes of excavated material, the world's biggest shovels are needed to dig and load. Though these mining operations have been going on for the last few decades, recent advancements in the size of mining shovels and haulers have swayed many of the operations to increase the size of their big shovel/truck fleets, and move away from the more traditional use of draglines and bucket wheel excavators.

Even though large cable mining shovels are still the No. 1 choice of the mining industry for large-scale hard rock digging, the hydraulic shovels are beginning to catch up, both in size and reliability. The hydraulic machines, along with the largest wheel loaders from Caterpillar and LeTourneau, have severely cut into the cable shovel manufacturers' bottom line. While Bucyrus offers five shovel model lines, and P&H offers seven, almost all current

sales come from each company's two largest machines. When a shovel below 40 cubic yards is needed, chances are it will be for a hydraulic unit. And life is not going to get any easier for cable shovel manufacturers, with RH400-size excavators currently under development from Liebherr, Hitachi, and Komatsu Demag. All three companies have tentatively planned such product introductions in the year 2000.

Hitachi EX3500-3

Since its introduction in 1987, the Hitachi EX3500 hydraulic excavator has been a popular choice when it comes to large, hard-digging loading shovels. In March 1996, Hitachi introduced an upgraded model, the Super EX3500-3. This model is powered by two Cummins KT38-C925 engines, rated at 1,760 gross hp and 1,635 fhp. The EX3500-3 weighs in at 368 tons for the front shovel and carries a standard 23.5-cubic yard shovel bucket. This EX3500-3 is pictured working in December 1996 at a Black Beauty coal mine in southern Indiana. *ECO*

Hitachi EX2500

Introduced at the March 1996 CONEXPO, the 18.3-cubic yard Hitachi EX2500 loading shovel is ideally suited for work in large-to-medium size mining operations. Power is supplied by a 16-cylinder, Cummins KTA50-C diesel engine, rated at 1,300 gross hp and 1,254 fhp. The machine's overall working weight is 264 tons, and the backhoe model has a working weight of 280 tons. This 18.1-cubic yard EX-2500 backhoe is pictured working in October 1998 at the P&M Kemmerer Mine in Wyoming. The Hitachi EX2500's main rivals are the Komatsu-Demag H255S, the Liebherr R994, and the O&K RH120C. *ECO*

Hitachi EX5500

Introduced in July 1998, the Hitachi Super EX5500 hydraulic excavator is the largest loading shovel the company has ever built as of 1999. Its two Cummins K1A50-C diesel engines combine for an impressive 2,600 gross hp and 2,500 fhp. A working weight of 570 tons and a bucket rating of 35.5 cubic yards firmly places the EX5500 in a very select group of large hydraulic mining shovels—the same league as the Komatsu-Demag H455S and the O&K RH200. The first unit pictured loading a 240-ton Titan T-2240 hauler in September 1998, belongs to North American Construction. It shows the shovel at its first working assignment at Syncrude's new Aurora Mine, located northeast of Mildred Lake, Alberta. *Hitachi*

4 CRAWLER DOZERS

When it comes to crawler dozers, one immediately thinks of Caterpillar as the product leader—and rightly so. After all, Caterpillar is the largest producer of track-type tractors in the world. The company dates back to 1925, when the two competing firms of the Holt Tractor Co. and the C. L. Best Tractor Co. merged to form the Caterpillar Tractor Co. The Caterpillar trademark name had already been registered by Benjamin Holt with the U.S. Patent Office in 1910. But as early as November 1904, the Caterpillar term had been used in association with Holt's No. 77 wheel-type steamer prototype, whose rear wheels had been replaced with a set of tracks. Additional prototypes of the tracked steamer were built, and at the end of 1906, the seventh Holt Brothers Paddle Wheel Improved Traction Engine No. 111 was sold to a paying customer. This was Holt's first true production model of a tracked crawler tractor. In 1908, the gasoline engine was introduced on the Holt Model 40. Soon thereafter, steam-powered tractors would become quaint antiques.

In the following years, certain industry design achievements set the stage for the creation of large crawler dozers. In 1928, R. G. LeTourneau introduced his engine-driven, tractor-mounted cable "Power Control Unit," or PCU, for use on one of his early pulled-scraper designs. It proved so successful that cable control became standard on all his earth-moving inventions. Then, in 1932, LeTourneau started production of bulldozer blades; it was just one year after Caterpillar introduced its first diesel engine crawler, the Model Diesel Sixty.

LeTourneau began designing his large bulldozer and angledozer blades specially for Caterpillar tractors, and his heavy-duty PCU cable control was exactly what the market wanted. By 1934, LeTourneau had established agreements with most of the Caterpillar dealers to carry and market LeTourneau's tractor accessories and attachments, such as bulldozers, scrapers, rooters, wagons, and PCU controls. All of these were a perfect match for Caterpillar's crawler tractors, since Caterpillar was only building these units as bare machines. The Cat dealers were still allowed to sell other makes of blades and equipment, but the marriage of LeTourneau earth-moving equipment and Caterpillar's crawler tractors was truly a match made in heaven. Sales soared for both companies. Caterpillar crawlers were becoming better known as construction earth-moving machines and less as agricultural farm equipment. During World War II, the Caterpillar crawler tractor, pulling a Carryall scraper and equipped with a LeTourneau bulldozer blade, was a common sight. Other manufacturers had blades mounted on Cat tractors, but the LeTourneau models were far and away the most popular.

But even a strong marriage may falter. In February 1944, the alliance between LeTourneau and Caterpillar was terminated. In May 1944, Caterpillar announced that it was going to start building its own designs of bulldozer blades, scrapers, controls, etc., for use on its crawler tractors. From this point on, the two companies would go their separate ways, but the era of the large diesel crawler dozer had begun.

For years, the Caterpillar D8 series was the workhorse of the earth-moving industry. Powerful and reliable, it had an enviable reputation. This model line started out for Caterpillar in 1933 with the introduction of the Diesel Seventy-Five. This was followed by

Komatsu D575A-2 SD

A massive 90-cubic yard capacity wall of steel—25 feet, 3 inches wide and 10 feet, 8 inches high—that is the Komatsu D575A-2 SD. With such a mammoth blade and 1,150 fhp available from its 12-cylinder diesel, the D575A-2 SD is designed for the highest-volume production dozing operations. And with an operating weight of 316,200 pounds, or 158 tons, the Super-Dozer certainly has the bulk to cut the big jobs down to size. *ECO*

Caterpillar D9D

In 1955, Caterpillar introduced the dozer that set an industry standard for two decades—the mighty D9. Released as the D9D, this unit produced 286 fhp from its Cat D353 diesel engine and weighed in at approximately 72,395 pounds equipped with a U-blade. But by mid-1959, power had increased to 335 fhp in the D9E variant. Pictured in January 1956 is a Cat D9D (18A) tractor with a rare 24-foot-wide Balderson U-blade, specially designed for coal stockpiling operations at Ohio Power Company's Beverl plant. *Ohio Machinery*

the RD-8 in late 1935, and then the D8 in late 1937. Soon other manufacturers would challenge the Cat D8's status in the industry. In 1947, Allis-Chalmers introduced its 163-fhp HD-19H crawler dozer. This challenge was quickly met and surpassed by International Harvester in 1947 with its TD-24 dozer, rated at an industry-topping 180 fhp. Not to be outdone, Allis-Chalmers shot back in 1954 with its popular HD-21, rated at 204 fhp. But the HD-21's reign as the most powerful dozer available in the earth-moving industry would be a short one. Two companies were about to release crawler dozers that would chart a new course for the development of the large bulldozer. They were the Caterpillar D9D series, and the Twin-Power Euclid TC-12.

Starting in 1954 with the prototype D9X, and followed in 1955 by the first production D9D, no other dozer ever made a larger impact in the heavy construction and mining industry than this one. The Cat D9 series would set the standard against which all other large crawler dozers would be judged. The first D9D model was rated as a 286-fhp dozer. But by 1958, this had risen to 320 fhp. In 1959, an improved D9E series was released with new power ratings of 335 fhp. In 1961, the D9E was upgraded to the very popular D9G series, truly one of the greatest dozer models of the 1960s.

As Caterpillar was working on the development of the D9 series, the Euclid Division of General Motors Corporation was preparing the release of its big dozer—the TC-12. Even though Euclid TC-12 prototype dozers were operating in 1954, the machine did not get its final sheet metal form until

Euclid TC-12

The year 1955 saw the introduction of the world's first production "superdozer," the twin-engine Euclid TC-12. Equipped with two six-cylinder Detroit Diesel 6-71 engines and twin Allison Torqmatic Transmissions, it was the most powerful and maneuverable crawler in its day. No other dozer looked quite like it. With its unique automotive styling, twin rear-mounted radiators, and yellow-green paint scheme, the "Euc" always stood out against its yellow-painted competition. The first variation, the TC-12-1, produced 388 gross hp and 365 fhp. This was later increased to 436 gross hp and 413 fhp. In 1958, an improved TC-12-2 version was introduced with increased power ratings of 454 gross hp and 425 fhp. Shown during 1959 is a TC-12-2 being put through its paces. The operating weight of this version is 96,050 pounds. *ECO Collection*

early 1955. The Euclid TC-12 was a more powerful alternative to the Caterpillar D9. With its twin engines that produced 388-gross hp and 365 fhp, it was the most powerful dozer in the world at the time, but it was also a more complicated and expensive machine for the customer to maintain. In late 1956, a more powerful TC-12-1 model was introduced, producing 436 gross hp and 413 fhp. Oddly enough, in 1958 this unit had its power ratings *decreased* to 431 gross hp and 402 fhp. But things were put right again in 1959 with the release of the improved TC-12-2, with an increased power output of 454 gross hp and 425 fhp.

In January 1966, the designation for the TC-12 changed to the 82-80 BA. The specifications remained unchanged. Euclid released another model of the dozer in late 1967, with the 82-80 DA. This version of the twin-engine dozer was the most powerful of the series, with 476 gross hp and 440 fhp on hand. From 1968 to 1974, the big dozer was sold as the Terex 82-80, after GM was forced to give up the Euclid name and trademark, along with the hauler product line in July 1968. But in 1974, GM pulled the plug on the big twin-engined dozer. The 82-80 was just too complicated for its own good, and its long-term reliability record was less than glowing. In all, 901 of the green TC-12/82-80 crawler dozers were built, including prototypes.

In 1970, the crown of the world's most powerful single crawler dozer passed from the Terex 82-80 to the record-breaking Allis-Chalmers HD-41. With a power output of 524 fhp, it was the first crawler dozer to break the 500-horsepower barrier. Development on the big dozer can be traced to an early experimental 300-gross-hp Allis-Chalmers design dating back to 1955. This was followed by a dual-engine, 570-gross-hp and 500-fhp design in 1962 which was first publicly seen at the February 1963 Chicago Road Show. But numerous reliability and performance problems doomed this particular version. Starting in mid-1963, a redesigned HD-41 prototype was built, utilizing a single 540-gross-hp diesel engine, but problems persisted in this design as well. In late 1965, an improved HD-41 Phase I prototype showed great promise, and six test units were built. Information gained from these trials was incorporated into three 529-fhp, preproduction test machines—these started development in mid-1967, with all units in test programs by July 1969. The HD-41 finally became a production reality in 1970.

Terex 82-80
Euclid changed the model designation of its TC-12 dozer to the Euclid 82-80 in January 1966. The first variation produced was the 82-80 BA, which was in production from 1966 through 1967. It had the same horsepower ratings as the previous TC-12 it replaced. In late 1967, the 82-80 DA model was introduced. This version had upgraded twin Detroit Diesel 6-71N engines producing 476 gross hp and 440 fhp. In July 1968, General Motors was forced to give up its Euclid hauler line and the Euclid name and trademarks because of an antitrust investigation by the U.S. Justice Department. A new division name of "Terex" was selected in October 1968. From this point on, until the unit ceased production in 1974, the dozer was known as the Terex 82-80. Specifications remained the same as the last Euclid DA version. The operating weight for this unit was approximately 101,125 pounds with a ripper. *ECO Collection.*

Allis-Chalmers HD-41
The first production crawler dozer to break the 500-horsepower barrier was the Allis-Chalmers HD-41. This massive dozer produced 524 fhp from its 12-cylinder Cummins VT-1710-C diesel engine. With a 144,030-pound operating weight, the HD-41 could move tremendous amounts of earth. Its full U-blade was 20 feet wide and had a 28-cubic yard capacity. The HD-41 actually dates back to an experimental 300-horsepower Allis-Chalmers dozer from 1955. A two-engined HD-41 prototype made its first public showing at the February 1963 Road Show in Chicago. After several more years of prototype test tractors, a single-engine production version was officially released in 1970. *Dale Davis Collection*

When the Fiat and Allis-Chalmers construction equipment divisions were merged into a single company in January 1974, the HD-41 became the Fiat-Allis 41-B, though it was still marketed as the HD-41 in Europe. Power ratings remained unchanged. In late 1982, the 41-B model was upgraded to the Fiat-Allis FD50 model, which incorporated a dual power range of 525 fhp, and 550 fhp at higher ground speeds. By the early 1990s, Fiat was experiencing financial problems, and the FD50 was history.

Other notable powerful dozers in production during the time of the 41-B/FD50 model were the 425-fhp Fiat-Allis 31 in

1976, the 455-fhp FD40 in 1982, and the 475-fhp FD40B in 1989.

During the 1970s, Komatsu introduced two large dozers in North America, the D355A-3 in 1974 and the massive D455A-1 in 1975. The Komatsu D355A-3 dozer with its 410-fhp power rating was marketed to potential Caterpillar D9G/H customers, while the 620-fhp-rated D455A-1's target was the Fiat-Allis 41-B. And for a brief time in earth-moving history, the D455A-1 was the world's largest-production tracked dozer.

Despite the efforts of these competitors, Caterpillar held the top spot in the

Fiat-Allis FD50
The Fiat-Allis 41-B dozer was upgraded into the FD50 model in late 1982. New to this series of crawlers was the dual-power engine mode. This gave a horsepower rating of 525 fhp at normal operating speeds and 550 fhp at higher ground speeds from its Cummins VT-1710 diesel. The operating weight was increased to 161,594 pounds. The number of FD50 dozers sold in the United States was small, and the line was discontinued in the early 1990s. This FD50, shown in 1994, is pictured working in a coal mine in Ohio—it was purchased new back in 1983. *ECO*

Fiat-Allis 41-B
By January 1974, the Fiat and Allis-Chalmers construction equipment divisions were merged into a single company, Fiat-Allis. The designation of the HD-41 changed to the 41-B. The horsepower and engine choices were unchanged, but the operating weight was now up to a maximum of 160,000 pounds. The most obvious visual difference was the introduction of a new ROPS cab. Though the 41-B gained a reputation for having various electrical wiring problems and questionable final drive reliability, some mining operations had nothing but praise for this machine. Pictured is a 41-B in 1994, still in use, working reclamation duties at an eastern Ohio coal mine. This mine was one of the first to operate a fleet of original Allis-Chalmers HD-41 dozers back in 1970. *ECO*

Caterpillar D9H

The Caterpillar D9H series continued the success story firmly established by its predecessor, the D9G. The diesel engine remained the same, but more power was on tap with 410 fhp now available, and the operating weight increased to 107,230 pounds with ripper. Production on the D9H started in 1974 and ended in 1981. The D9H was the most powerful "low" sprocket drive dozer Caterpillar ever produced. *ECO*

Caterpillar Quad-Track DD9G

In late 1964, Cat released the first of its specialty high-production dozer combinations, the Quad-Track D9G. The engines were the same as in the standard D9G, producing a total of 770 fhp, and the combined operating weight was 175,000 pounds. In 1968, Caterpillar changed the designation of the Quad-Track to the Cat DD9G. In 1974, it was replaced by the DD9H version, which was in production until 1980. The H model was basically the same as the G set, with an increased power output of 820 fhp. The weight had also increased to 178,000 pounds. The Quad-Track dozer concept was originally conceived in 1963 by R. A. "Buster" Peterson of Peterson Tractor in California. Peterson built Quads for Caterpillar until 1968. In all, a total of 10 Peterson Quad-Tracks, 51 Cat DD9Gs, and 7 Cat DD9H sets were produced. An unknown number of field conversion in kits for use with used D9 tractors were also sold by Peterson. The DD9G shown was photographed in December 1993, working in northern Kentucky in subfreezing weather. *ECO*

large dozer marketplace with its D9 series throughout the 1960s and 1970s. The D9G and its D9H replacement in 1974 have often been referred to as the greatest bulldozers ever built. Caterpillar also offered these D9 models in special tandem tractor units. The first to be marketed by the company was the Quad-Track D9G in late 1964. This dual setup was introduced by Caterpillar to improve scraper cycle times and productivity. A Quad-Track D9G could obtain shorter push times, faster return speeds, and easier repositioning. The Quad-Track

was actually conceived of by R. A. "Buster" Peterson, of Peterson Tractor Co., a Caterpillar dealer in San Leandro, California, in 1963. All of the early Quad-Track D9G dozers were built by Peterson. From 1964 to 1968, Caterpillar marketed the quad dozers and had them prepared by Peterson. After Caterpillar bought the patents from Peterson for the quad-track attachment designs, it started building its own quad-sets, now referred to as the DD9G. The 770-fhp DD9G was produced from 1968 to 1974, when it was upgraded into the 820-fhp DD9H

model. Production on this version ended in 1980. Caterpillar also produced side-by-side D9 dozer combinations, fitted with a special 24-foot-wide bulldozing blade. These were the SxS D9G from 1969 to 1974, and the SxS D9H from 1974 to 1977.

In late 1977, Caterpillar introduced the first of its "high sprocket drive" dozers—the legendary D10. Even though the high sprocket design had previously been seen in such machines as the 1917 Leader tractor, or the Cletrac Model F of 1920, it took Cat engineering know-how to turn the concept

Caterpillar SxS D9H

Another of Caterpillar's specialty crawler dozers was its powerful SxS D9H. With a horsepower rating of 820 fhp, it was even more powerful than a D10, a D11N or an early D11R. Only the updated D11R, which began service in mid-1997, and the D11R CD are more powerful. Once again, the engines were the same as in the standard D9H and the DD9H quad-track unit— six-cylinder Cat D353 diesel engines. With a special 9U bulldozing blade that was 24 feet wide and 7 feet tall, the SxS excelled at high-volume bulldozing in coal stripping applications, such as overburden removal, stockpiling, and land reclamation. Its working weight was right around 190,500 pounds. The original 770 fhp Caterpillar SxS D9G was in production from 1969 to 1974, and the SxS D9H from 1974 to 1977. A total of 11 Cat SxS D9G sets and 13 Cat SxS D9H sets were factory-produced. *ECO*

into one of the most powerful production dozers of its time. The elevated track design of the D10 reduced the shock loads from ground contact, minimizing roller frame alignment problems and limiting the amount of debris that could damage the drive sprocket teeth. With 700 fhp available, the D10 took the title of world's most powerful track dozer away from the Komatsu D455A-1.

In 1986, Caterpillar introduced the updated model of its D10—the D11N. The D11N produced 770 fhp and has been considered one of the premier dozers of the 1980s and 1990s. The D11N was replaced by the D11R model in 1996. At first, power figures were unchanged, but in 1997 power was increased to 850 fhp.

As this century has drawn to a close, Komatsu has challenged the dominance of the Caterpillar D11N/D11R model lines with its big D475A dozers. The D475A-1 series was introduced in 1987 as a 740-fhp-rated machine. In 1989, this power figure was raised to 770 fhp with the release of an improved D475A-2 model. This dozer has been a strong seller for Komatsu, though its sales have not approached its counterpart from Caterpillar. To meet the challenge of the more powerful D11R, Komatsu announced

Caterpillar SxS D9H "Double Dude"

Probably the most famous dozer ever to push a yard of dirt was Russell & Sons Construction Company's "Double Dude," built in the late 1970s. In order to create it, a 48-foot-wide bulldozer blade was fabricated by Balderson (referred to by Balderson as a BRAP III Land Reclamation Plow) to fit a pair of Caterpillar SxS D9Hs set at about a 45-degree angle. To make this possible, the dozers were offset to each other, and a special rear tie-bar was constructed. Also, the air-over-hydraulic lines were routed in a sling arrangement between the two tractors. The engine power was left at 820 fhp, the same as in the standard Cat dozer. The unit was capable of moving up to 14,000 cubic yards of material per hour. The "Double Dude" is no longer in service, mainly due to changes in mining regulations, and it remains the only one ever constructed. Russell also built a 60-foot-wide blade, connected it to two Fiat-Allis 41-B dozers, and called it "Big Daddy," but this design proved too difficult to maneuver while working. *Russell & Sons*

Caterpillar D10N

Released in 1987, the Cat D10N replaced the D9L model, which had been in service since 1980. It had the same Cat 3412 diesel engine as its predecessor, but horsepower ratings were increased to 557 gross hp and 520 fhp. The operating weight was also up, listed at 147,405 pounds, with a ripper. A larger 28.7-cubic -yard capacity blade was standard, measuring 17 feet, 3 inches wide and 7 feet high. The big D10N was well liked in mining operations worldwide. *ECO*

in 1999 an upgraded model of its big mining dozer—the 860 fhp D475A-3 SD.

Marketed alongside the D475A series dozer is Komatsu's gigantic D575A-2 SD. Introduced in 1995, it is the largest-production crawler dozer available to the mining industry, as of 1999. The development of this mammoth crawler dates back to the February 1981 Conexpo in Houston, Texas. There, Komatsu unveiled an experimental prototype dozer called the D555A. Producing 1,000 fhp, it had the potential to give Caterpillar's D10 a run for its money. But this was also a time of worsening worldwide economics. The recession of the early 1980s stopped the giant D555A dozer cold in its tracks.

Eventually, starting in 1986, the prototype was rebuilt, improved, and introduced into testing in 1989 as the D575A-1. Information gathered from the D575A-1 was incorporated into the full-production D575A-2 model, rated at 1,050 fhp, in 1991. After a short stay working in a Pennsylvania coal mine, the first production unit was shipped to a customer in Las Vegas, Nevada, to be utilized as a big-production ripping dozer. In 1995, an additional model of the big crawler was introduced by Komatsu as the D575A-2 SD. The "SD" stands for "Super-Dozer," an apt title for a machine

continued on page 84

Caterpillar D10R

In 1996, Caterpillar replaced the D10N with an improved model, the D10R. The D10R is powered by a Cat 3412E diesel engine, rated at 613 gross hp and 570 fhp. The operating weight is 144,986 pounds. Its standard U blade is the same as the previous D10N model. One of the D10R dozer's key features is its electronic steering and transmission control, which can be operated with one hand, thus increasing comfort and lessening fatigue for the operator. *ECO*

Caterpillar D10

In late 1977, Caterpillar introduced the dozer that would turn the market upside-down and change the look of all its large dozers for years to come —the legendary D10. With its elevated track design and mammoth blade, it completely distinguished itself from its competition. The elevated drive sprocket design was not necessarily new to the earth-moving industry, but Caterpillar was able to take the concept and apply it effectively in one of the world's largest-production dozers. Powered by a 12-cylinder Cat D348 diesel engine, the dozer had a rating of 700 fhp. With an operating weight of 191,936 pounds, no job was too big for this monster. Its 10U blade was 20 feet wide and 7 feet high, with a capacity to move up to 35 cubic yards of material. Early versions of the D10 had only a single exhaust stack, while later versions had dual exhaust. *Caterpillar.*

Caterpillar D11N

In 1986, Caterpillar released its updated version of the ground-breaking D10, the D11N. Without a doubt, the D11N is one of the most popular large dozers ever produced. It may no longer hold the title of the world's largest production bulldozer, but it's hard to find a large mining operation that is not operating these giants. With an 11U bulldozer blade that is 21 feet wide and 7 feet, 7 inches high, and rated at a large 45-cubic yard capacity, it can move tremendous amounts of material economically. Another improvement on the D11N is its extended roller and track frames, which increase the contact length area of the tracks. A new eight-cylinder Cat 3508 diesel engine powers the big crawler with ratings of 817 gross hp and 770 fhp. The weight was 214,847 pounds with a single shank ripper. *ECO*

Caterpillar D11R CD
Caterpillar replaced the popular D11N with the improved D11R model series in March 1996. At the September 1996 MINExpo in Las Vegas, Nevada, a special dozer based on this new crawler was unveiled, the Caterpillar D11R CD Carrydozer. The Carrydozer is powered by a Cat 3508B diesel engine, rated at 915 gross hp and 850 fhp. Unique to this dozer is its 57-cubic yard blade. Designed to carry material inside the blade curvature, this increases the effective weight of the tractor and enables it to push a larger pile of earth in front of the dozer. Its blade is 22 feet wide and 10 feet, 8 inches tall. The working weight of the Carrydozer is 239,550 pounds, compared to the standard D11R's 225,500 pounds. The standard D11R model was fitted with the Carrydozer's engine and power ratings in August 1997. The Carrydozer was officially released for sale by Caterpillar in April 1998. *Caterpillar.*

Continued from page 81

rated at 1,150 fhp and capable of wielding a massive 90-cubic yard capacity blade, which is more than 24 feet wide. The SD version also has a specially designed front end for supporting the blade control cylinders and an improved undercarriage, which is balanced for dozing operations. The earlier D575A-2 versions are now referred to as SR models, meaning "Super-Ripper." The unit originally shipped to Nevada in 1993 is now considered a D575A-2 SR.

Not every powerful dozer has come from Caterpillar or Komatsu. Other powerful machines were conceived of and built by individuals without the backing of the traditional powers of equipment supply—these were the diesel-electric drive Doerr-Tractor from Charles Doerr of Canada and the ACCO Dozer from Umberto Acco of Italy. Production started on the Doerr-Tractor in November 1964 with the one-and-only unit delivered into service in 1966, for Mannix Company Limited's Alberta Coal, Ltd. Built around an articulated chassis, utilizing four complete Euclid TC-12 crawler assemblies, the dozer looked much like a quad Cat D9G. It was powered by two Cummins engines, developing

Komatsu D355A-3
In 1974, Komatsu, Ltd., of Japan introduced a competitor to Caterpillar's successful D9 series, the Komatsu D355A-3 dozer. Powered by Komatsu's own six-cylinder SA6D155-4A diesel engine, it equaled the power of the D9 with 410 fhp. The Komatsu was no lightweight either, tipping the scales at 121,150 pounds. With a 15-foot-wide blade, the dozer had the capacity to move up to 22 cubic yards of material. No longer in production, its spot in the current Komatsu lineup is now occupied by the D375A-3. *Urs Peyer*

Facing page

Komatsu D375A-3
The year 1996 saw the introduction of the redesigned Komatsu D375A-3. The D375A series was introduced in late 1987 as a 508-fhp, 125,890-pound dozer. The D375A-3 series is powered by a Komatsu SA6D170E diesel engine, rated at 573 gross hp and 525 fhp and has an operating weight of 149,180 pounds. The blade capacity is 28.8 cubic yards, which puts it in the same class as the Cat D10R. *KMS*

Komatsu D455A-1

In 1975, Komatsu released what it called the world's first superdozer, the D455A. With a power rating of 620 fhp, it was the most powerful dozer one could buy and was squarely aimed at the American mining market. High production was what this dozer was all about. With a 20-foot wide, 42-cubic yard capacity blade, this dozer could really cut the big jobs down to size. The dozer was powerful, tough and reliable; it earned its reputation in some of the most abrasive working conditions in the field. Pictured is the upgraded version of the D455A-1—improved with more power available from its 650-fhp, 12-cylinder Cummins VTA1710-C800 diesel engine and a new ROPS cab. The big machine weighed in at a hefty 182,175 pounds. *Komatsu Ltd.*

Komatsu D475A-2

Released in 1987, the D475A-1 was Komatsu's answer to Caterpillar's D11N dozer. The original dozer was powered by an 8-cylinder Komatsu SA8V170 diesel engine, producing 740 fhp. In 1989, an even more powerful version of the crawler was released, the D475A-2. With a new 12-cylinder Komatsu SA12V140 diesel engine, power was increased to 770 fhp. The weight of the big crawler is 214,740 pounds. Both versions utilize a 45-cubic yard capacity blade that measures 20 feet, 4 inches wide and 8 feet, 7 inches high. Shown here is a D475A-2 model, working at a West Virginia coal mine in 1997. *ECO*

1,050 gross hp and 984 fhp, delivered through four GE traction motors. The Doerr-Tractor was 33 feet in length, while the Caterpillar Quad-Track D9G measured 42 feet, 6 inches. Both units weighed in at 88 tons fully operational.

The ACCO Dozer was introduced in 1980 and was displayed at the Verona trade show in Italy. The giant ACCO was powered by two Caterpillar diesel engines, producing a combined 1,300 gross hp. Weighing in at 183 tons, it is the world's largest crawler dozer. In comparison, the Komatsu D575A-2 SD weighs in at *only* 158 tons. The ACCO Dozer was specially built for a large earth-moving project in Libya, but the American trade sanctions on that country in the early 1980s doomed the final delivery of the giant. Today, it sits in front of ACCO's facilities in Italy—the only dozer of its type ever built.

Komatsu D475A-3SD
Pictured in December 1998, is the prototype Komatsu D475A-3 SD "Super Dozer," undergoing testing at a southern Indiana coal mine. Compared to the previous version, the D475A-3 SD is more powerful, with 860 fhp available from its new Komatsu SDA 12V140 diesel engine. The dozing blade is now 21 feet wide, with a 58.9-cubic yard rating. The overall working weight of the dozer is 230,380 pounds. *KMS*

Komatsu D555A
At the February 1981 Conexpo in Houston, Texas, Komatsu unveiled a mammoth experimental prototype dozer called the D555A. The weight of the big dozer was 132 tons or 264,550 pounds. It had ample power on hand, with a rating of 1,000 fhp. It also had a case of bad timing. With the worldwide economic recession in full swing, high interest rates, and low prices for raw minerals, buyers were in short supply. The big dozer would never find a home in its present form. It would have to wait until the end of the decade, to be reborn as the D575A-1. *Komatsu Ltd.*

Komatsu D575A-2 SR

In 1991, the first U.S. production D575A-2 SR started work in the same Pennsylvania coal mine where its prototype version had first undergone field testing in 1989 and 1990. After a short stay there, it was delivered to its new owners, American Asphalt & Grading Company, located in North Las Vegas, Nevada, in 1993. Currently, its main function is to rip the dense cap rock that surrounds Las Vegas. This rock can run as thick as three feet in places, and many areas are close to residential zones, where blasting is prohibited. With a maximum ripping depth of 6 feet, 9 inches and 1,050 fhp, the D575A-2 SR is well suited to this kind of task. The SR dozer's blade is rated at 70.8 cubic yards and is 22 feet, 4 inches wide. A D575A-2 SR is pictured working in September 1996, ripping in the Las Vegas area. *Urs Peyer*

Komatsu D575A-2 SD

When the going gets tough, the big get even bigger. Enter the Komatsu D575A-2 SD Super-Dozer, as of 1999 the world's largest-production crawler dozer. Introduced in 1995, the D575A-2 SD is powered by a 12-cylinder Komatsu SA12V170 diesel engine rated at 1,150 fhp. The SD version is equipped with a massive 90-cubic yard bulldozing blade and rear-mounted counterweights. Shown working in June 1997 are two of Princess Beverly Coal Company's D575A-2 SD dozers, pushing blasted overburden. As of 1998, Princess Beverly operates eight of these Super-Dozers at its Kayford and Notomine mountaintop coal mines near Cabin Creek, West Virginia. The company took delivery of its first D575A-2 SD for the Kayford Mine in February 1995. *ECO*

Dresser TD-40B

The Dresser Company purchased the construction equipment division of International Harvester in 1982, which had a solid history of making tough, dependable dozers. The tradition continued after the acquisition with the TD-40B, the largest in a long line of TD machines that date back to the first IH diesel in 1933. Introduced around 1989, it is powered by a six-cylinder Cummins KTA-19C diesel engine with a horsepower rating of 520 fhp. The operating weight is 141,000 pounds, and its standard blade is 16 feet wide with a 24.8-cubic yard capacity. This model replaced the original TD-40, introduced in 1985, which had a 460-fhp power rating and a weight of 134,000 pounds. An upgraded TD-40C model was released in 1997 with a new ROPS cab. Today, the Dresser TD series of dozers is built in Poland. *ECO*

ACCO Dozer

The giant ACCO Dozer is one of the largest, most powerful—and underused—crawler dozers of all time. The dozer was built by Umberto Acco at his construction and fabricating company in Italy in 1980, and was officially unveiled at the Verona trade show. The machine had many notable features, including side-by-side-mounted Caterpillar V-8 diesel engines rated at 1,300 gross hp and a high track configuration, driven by an upper and lower sprocket on each side. The dozer carried a blade that was 23 feet wide and 9 feet high. The total weight of the unit was 183 tons. Originally built for a Libyan earth-moving project, trading restrictions caused the cancellation of the order. The dozer is shown sitting on display at Acco's equipment lot in October 1997, with little hope of ever going to work. *Klaus Mayr*

5 WHEEL LOADERS AND DOZERS

Large rubber-tired wheel loaders, or tractor shovels as they were once more commonly known, are a relatively recent innovation in earth moving. The first integrated front-end wheel loader, built from the ground up as a wheel loader, was invented by Frank G. Hough in 1939. Referred to as the Hough Model HS, but also known as the "Hough Small," it was a humble sort of machine that looked more like a forklift with a bucket than the machines we are accustomed to seeing today. But Hough's little 1/3-cubic yard capacity invention was literally the starting point of the modern wheel loader and the material handling industry. Before the Hough Small, early front end loaders were cable-operated attachments mounted on existing agricultural tractors. Other models followed, but two early units stand out as being true trendsetters for the industry. These were the 1.5-cubic yard Hough HM in 1947, and the 4-cubic yard HW in 1950. The model HM was the first hydraulic front-end loader to incorporate four-wheel drive. The larger model HW was the first loader to have planetary axles, a power-shift transmission, and a torque converter. All of these features can be found on today's large mechanical-drive wheel loaders. In 1952, the Frank G. Hough Co. became a subsidiary of International Harvester Company. This allowed the Hough wheel loaders to be marketed from a much broader dealer network, further establishing the front-end loader's presence in the earth-moving industry.

Still, one key design innovation, central to *all* of today's modern large machines, lay undiscovered. Articulated steering, the ability of the front and rear sections of a vehicle to pivot on a hinge, dramatically increased the mobility (and popularity) of large wheel loaders. The honor of its invention goes to Mixermobile Manufacturers Inc., with the introduction of its Scoopmobile Model LD-5 in 1953. The Model LD-5 was the world's first articulated frame steering, four-wheel drive wheel loader. But the Scoopmobile's Swivel-Steer models did not catch on in the earth-moving industry at first. There were engineering problems that needed to be addressed, and the industry took a wait-and-see attitude toward the pivot-steering concept as a whole.

In the early 1960s, established manufacturers of wheel loaders started to introduce new articulated-steering, four-wheel drive models. Euclid Division of GM was the first to offer a full line of production machines in January 1962. After Euclid came model introductions from Caterpillar in 1963, Hough in 1964, and both Clark Michigan and Allis-Chalmers in 1965. New designs of pivot-steering machines soon pushed any remaining rear-wheel steering models out of the picture. The first of the big articulated-steering wheel loaders was the Caterpillar 988, introduced in early 1963. Caterpillar had originally entered the wheel loader market in 1959 with its No. 944A, but the Cat 988 was the company's first pivot-steer model. The 988 was powered by a Cat Diesel engine, rated at 375 gross hp and 300 fhp. The standard bucket capacity was five to six cubic yards, with a 17,500-pound load limit. The 988 series

LeTourneau L-1800 Letro-Loader
The LeTourneau L-1800 comes equipped with standard 50/80-57,68PR(L-4)-size tires, or 53.5/85-57,68PR(L-5) units for extreme service use. These are among the latest, most technologically advanced and largest tires the industry has to offer. The L-1800 is 58 feet, 6 inches long and 21 feet wide. The loader has a maximum bucket height of almost 40 feet, 8 inches with its high-lift attachment. This white L-1800, working at Powder River Coal's Rochelle Mine in July 1996, is equipped with a 36-cubic yard rock bucket, high-lift arms, and a Cummins 2,000-fhp engine. In October 1998, this L-1800 was equipped with a massive new 55-cubic yard coal-loading bucket, the largest in the world for a wheel loader. *ECO*

has been continually updated and improved over the years, and as of 1999 is still offered in the company's product line.

In 1964, the Frank G. Hough Co. introduced its 10-cubic yard capacity H-400 PAY Loader. The H-400 was a big articulated loader based on Hough's popular D-500 PAY Dozer. Power from the loader's Cummins diesel was a healthy 525 gross hp and 421 fhp. The maximum bucket capacity was 30,000 pounds.

In 1965, Scoopmobile muscled its way into the big loader market with the Swivel-Steer Model 1200. The big Scoopmobile was powered by a Cummins diesel, rated at 525 gross hp and 504 fhp. The loader's standard 10-cubic yard Roll-Out Bucket was rated at 37,000 pounds. But this rating came at a price. The Model 1200 suffered from many developmental "gremlins" that plagued the loader throughout its career. After the Scoopmobile product line became part of WABCO in 1968, the power output was reduced to 500 gross hp and 478 fhp in hopes of improving drivetrain reliability. The maximum load rating was also reduced to 30,000 pounds, but bucket capacity remained at 10 cubic yards.

WABCO eventually built its first Model 1200 in February 1970, but it was too little, too late. The Model 1200's out-of-date design didn't allow it to compete with the newer wheel loader designs coming into the market.

Between 1965 and 1966, two large wheel loader models were launched that pushed the size and performance envelope of hydraulic, mechanical-drive loaders. The first of these was the 12-cubic yard Michigan 475A Series III, from Clark Equipment Company. The Michigan 475A was the largest wheel loader offered at the time by

Dart 600C

The Unit Rig Dart 600C was the last version of the popular 600-series wheel loader to be produced. The model was introduced as the KW-Dart D600 in late 1965, with the first unit put into service in 1966. In the field, the mechanical-drive Dart 600C was instantly recognizable because of its offset cab, which provided increased operator visibility while loading. No other production loader had this feature. The standard bucket capacity for the Dart 600C was 16 cubic yards, with a 48,000-pound load rating. The most powerful engines offered were either a 875-gross-hp Detroit Diesel 12V-149TB, or a 860-gross-hp Cummins KT-38C. Maximum operating weight was 203,700 pounds. This loader was also built and sold in Canada under the Sicard name in the late 1960s. Pictured is a 600C, equipped with the optional 23-cubic yard coal ejector bucket, at P&M's Kemmerer Mine in southwestern Wyoming. *Terex*

Dresser 580 PAY Loader

The International-Hough Division of the International Harvester Co. unveiled its experimental prototype, 18-cubic yard capacity 580 PAY Loader at the 1971 American Mining Congress (AMC) show. But it was not until the October 1978 AMC show that a production version would officially be introduced. The early 580 was powered by a Detroit Diesel 12V-149TI engine, rated at 1,200 gross hp and 1,075 fhp. The standard bucket capacity was 22 cubic yards, with a maximum 66,000-pound load rating. The length of the 580 PAY Loader was 48 feet, with a 20-foot width; it had a 281,000-pound operating weight. *ECO*

KDC Haulpak 4000

In early 1991, the Komatsu Dresser Company, then a 50/50 joint venture formed in 1988 from both the Komatsu and Dresser companies' construction divisions, released the 4000-series loader. Marketed by its Haulpak division and looking much like the old 580 model it replaced, the Haulpak 4000 was bigger and more powerful. Engine choices were either a Detroit Diesel 12V-149TI DDEC, rated at 1,350 gross hp and 1,280 fhp, or a Cummins KTTA-38-C, rated at 1,310 gross hp and 1,250 fhp. The standard bucket capacity had also been increased to 24 cubic yards, with a 72,000-pound load limit. The operating weight was 343,597 pounds. With a longer wheel base than the old 580, length had increased to 53 feet, 8 inches. Early units, such as the one shown here, were fitted with 49.5-57,68PR tires, but later models received the improved, wider 50/80-57,68PR versions. Early in 1995, the Haulpak 4000 wheel loader was discontinued, bringing the long history of the International/Hough/Dresser 580 machines to an end. *KMS*

Clark, whose product line dated back to 1954. The prototype unit made its appearance in late 1965, with the first production loader delivered into service in 1966. Power output from the 475A's Cummins diesel was 635 gross hp and 554 fhp. The maximum load capacity was 36,000 pounds.

The other loader, which was released about the same time, was the KW-Dart D600 model. KW-Dart had performed some early wheel loader tests with a rigid-frame prototype "test-mule" in Pennsylvania in the early 1960s. Early concept features were refined into an articulated, offset cab model called the D600, which was announced in 1965. The first unit, delivered into service in 1966, carried a standard 15-cubic yard rock bucket with a 45,000-pound load limit. The standard Cummins diesel gave the loader 700 gross hp, which was increased in later versions. Other models that followed the D600 were the D600 Series B in 1973, the 600C in 1978, and the 600E Ejector Bucket Loader in 1982. By 1982, the regular Model 600C was also now rated as a 48,000-pound, 16-cubic yard capacity machine. Over the next few years, the Dart loaders were built in ever smaller numbers until the last unit, a rebuilt 600C, left the Unit Rig Tulsa plant in 1995. Still, over 400 Dart loaders were eventually sold.

The next big wheel loader release was Caterpillar's 992 model. It was without a doubt the best-selling and most popular articulated 10- to 15-cubic yard loader series ever offered by any manufacturer. The first Cat 992 prototype loader started field testing in late 1965, and was joined by additional preproduction units in 1966. The 992 series was officially introduced in 1968. This 550-fhp loader was initially rated as a 10-cubic yard, 30,000-pound capacity machine, but its capabilities were enhanced in 1973 and in 1977, with the advent of the 992B and C models. The 992C in particular was an industry favorite. With 735 gross hp and 690 fhp, the 992C had the muscle to take on the really big jobs. The redesigned lift arms on the loader allowed the 992C to be equipped with a 12.5-cubic yard bucket, rated at 37,500 pounds. It was not until 15 years later, in 1992, that Caterpillar finally upgraded the 992C into the 14-cubic yard 992D. The power of the new model remained unchanged until 1996, when it was increased to 755 gross hp and 710 fhp. In September 1996, Caterpillar unveiled the next step in the evolution of its most popular large loader series—the 992G. The power of the G model was up to 880 gross hp and 800 fhp, with a standard bucket capacity of 16 cubic yards. But the key design feature of the new loader was its one-piece, box-section, front lift arm design. In March 1997, the 992G was officially released for sale.

In the early 1970s, wheel loader evolution took a big jump up in overall machine size and load capacities. In 1971, International-Hough previewed an experimental 18-cubic yard wheel loader called the 580 PAY Loader. But it would not be until 1978 that a full-production loader was finally released for sale to the mining industry. By this time, the capacity of the loader had grown to 22 cubic yards, with a 66,000-pound load rating. Its single Detroit Diesel engine produced 1,200 gross hp and 1,075 fhp. Just as the 580 model was getting established in the industry, it slammed right into the early 1980s' economic recession, which almost brought production to a standstill.

But International Harvester had invested too much in the 580 program to give up on it just yet. In 1982, Dresser Industries acquired the construction division of International Harvester, and around 1985, the International-Hough reference was dropped in favor of the Dresser name. In 1988, Komatsu and Dresser Industries formed a 50/50 joint venture company with their construction equipment divisions, called the Komatsu Dresser Company, or KDC for short. Despite these changes in ownership, the 580 design remained unaffected. Sales of the loader started to pick up in the late 1980s,

Clark Michigan 675 Prototype
Without a doubt, the most famous wheel loader ever built was the Clark Michigan 675. The big Michigan pushed the technological boundaries that had limited large wheel loaders to 12- to 15-cubic yard capacities. With a 24-cubic yard bucket carrying a rated capacity of 72,000 pounds, the 675 was the largest loader produced up to that point. The first prototype 675, shown here in the summer of 1970, was equipped with two GM Detroit Diesel 16V-71N-65 engines, rated at 1,270 gross hp and 1,144 fhp combined. The operating weight was 350,000 pounds. It was also equipped with Goodyear 36.00-51,58PR(L-4) tires, which proved to be totally inadequate for a loader of its size. That would soon change, but at the time they were the largest pieces of rubber around. *ECO Collection*

Clark Michigan 675

The Michigan engineers were well aware of the problems encountered in the early 675 units. In September 1975, the improved Lot-3 version was introduced with more power available from upgraded dual Cummins VTA-1710-C700 engines, rated at 1,400 gross hp and 1,316 fhp. Other improvements included the introduction of a large hydraulic oil cooler mounted over the right rear wheel, a beefed up transmission, and more-durable clutch plates and hydraulic cylinders. But the biggest problem was extreme tire wear on the Michelins. In 1976, Goodyear introduced the world's largest tire, the massive 67-51SXT,54PR(L-5) series; it was the answer to the world's largest wheel loader tire problem. This raised the operating weight to 389,600 pounds. Pictured in August 1978 is a 675 with the massive 67-inch Goodyears, operated by Green Coal Company in western Kentucky. *ECO Collection*

Clark Michigan 675

The Clark Michigan 675 loader dimensions were very similar to machines currently offered by other manufacturers today. The overall length of the 675 was 53 feet, with a 19-foot, 8-inch width. In all, a total of 18 serial-numbered machines were produced—two prototypes and 14 production versions. Of course, this only adds up to 16 units. The last two 675 loaders were remanufactured early versions. They were rebuilt from the ground up and updated to 675C specifications, with new power ratings of 1,350 gross hp and 1,270 fhp and new serial numbers. The working weight was raised to 389,500 pounds. These last two units were delivered in 1988, along with all the spare parts available to NERCO's Spring Creek Coal Mine in Montana. After this, the book was closed on the 675 loader program. *ECO Collection*

which gave the model line new hope. In 1991, the 580 loader was transformed into the Dresser 4000. The 4000 wheel loader produced more power, with 1,350 gross hp and 1,280 fhp now available. Standard bucket capacity was increased to 24 cubic yards, with a 72,000-pound, maximum load limit. But the 4000 could not reach sufficient sales, and Komatsu killed the 4000 product line in 1995, bringing the Hough/International/Dresser 580 story to an end.

Perhaps the most famous wheel loader of all time was Clark Equipment's Michigan 675 model. It was not necessarily more productive, reliable, or sales prolific than its competing loaders, but the Michigan 675 had something that few of its contemporaries possessed—presence, and lots of it. During its day, the big Michigan was the most powerful and largest-capacity wheel loader in the world.

The prototype 675 started testing at the Clark factory proving ground in the summer of 1970. This first unit was powered by a pair of Detroit Diesel engines, rated at 1,270 gross hp and 1,144 fhp. The bucket capacity was 24 cubic yards, with a 72,000-pound load limit. During the prototype testing, it became apparent that the GM engines were not well suited for life in an ultra-large wheel loader.

Nor were the tires, deemed totally unsuitable for a machine of the 675's weight and intended working environment. Even though the Goodyear 36.00x51 tires were the largest tires then available to the industry for use in loader applications, they were still just standard off-highway truck tires, and their life span on the 675 was a sorry 200 to 300 hours tops. More than anything else, this slowed development of the large loader program.

During 1972, a second prototype was built, this one powered by two VTA-1710-C635 Cummins engines, rated at 1,270 gross hp and 1,186 fhp combined. At this

continued on page 100

SMEC/Kawasaki 180t Loader

In 1986, the Surface Mining Equipment for Coal Technology Research Association (SMEC) of Japan, established in March 1983, released its first major product, the SMEC 180t super wheel loader. It was built primarily by Kawasaki Heavy Industries, Ltd., of Japan. The SMEC was powered by two Cummins VTA-28C, 12-cylinder diesel engines with a combined output of 1,341 fhp. The standard bucket capacity was 25 cubic yards, with a 77,000-pound load rating. The loader was 55 feet in length, with a 21-foot width. The tires were Bridgestone 67-51, 54PR(L-5) series, the same size as the discontinued Goodyears on the Clark Michigan 675C. The total operating weight was 396,720 pounds. The first unit started tests at a quarry owned by Okumura Gumi Civil Engineering Co., Ltd., on Nishijima Island, in 1987. From there, it was shipped to Australia for further testing. *Kawasaki Heavy Industries*

Komatsu WA800-2

Komatsu's large WA800 wheel loader series has been targeted directly at Caterpillar's 992, size class of machines, since the series was introduced in 1986. The WA800-2 is powered by a 12-cylinder Komatsu SA12V140Z-1 diesel engine, rated at 833 gross hp and 789 fhp. The standard bucket size is 13.7 cubic yards. The total operating weight of the WA800-2 is 219,200 pounds. An upgraded WA800-3 model was introduced in Japan and Australia in 1998, and in North America in 1999, with power ratings raised to 808 fhp. The capacity was also increased to 14.4 cubic yards. *ECO*

Komatsu WA900-1

The Komatsu WA900-1 wheel loader made its first public appearance at the September 1996 MINExpo in Las Vegas, Nevada. The WA900-1 shares most of its outside dimensions with its sister unit, the WA800-2. But the WA900-1 has a higher-power output Komatsu SA12V140Z-1 engine, with figures of 897 gross hp and 853 fhp. The bucket capacity is 17 cubic yards with an operating weight of 233,930 pounds. In 1999, an improved WA900-3 version was introduced. *ECO*

Previous pages

Caterpillar 994

In the late 1980s, rumors had persisted throughout the industry that Caterpillar was developing a very large wheel loader. In October 1990, Cat confirmed those rumors by introducing the giant 994, the largest wheel loader the company had ever manufactured and one of the largest in the world. The 994 is powered by a single Cat 3516, V-16 diesel engine, driving a Cat planetary power shift transmission. The entire drivetrain is of a mechanical nature, as opposed to the diesel electric-drive systems utilized in the large LeTourneau loaders. Power ratings for the 994 are 1,336 gross hp and 1,250 fhp. *ECO*

Continued from page96

same time, Michelin introduced the 50.5x51 XRD-2(L-5) tire for use on the 675, often referred to as the "banana" tread tire, but it could only manage 500 hours on average. Still, there was no other choice but the Michelins, and development of the 675 continued to revolve around these frequently changed tires for some time. In 1976, Goodyear introduced the tire the Michigan was meant to wear—the massive 67-51SXT, 54PR(L-5) series, then the world's largest tire. Clark started to upgrade loaders in the field with the new Goodyears as the old tires failed, first with the fronts, and then the rears. All loaders built after 1976 came standard with the new 67-inch tires.

In total, 18 Michigan 675 loaders were built—two prototypes and 14 regular production machines. Of course this totals only 16 units. Clark repurchased four loaders to rebuild into 675C series machines, all with new serial numbers, but only two were eventually remanufactured. The other two fell under the scrapper's cutting torch. One of the rebuilt units was shown at the 1981 Conexpo in Houston, Texas. This unit was eventually put into the local dealer's inventory, where it stayed for the next seven years. It was eventually sold along with the other rebuilt 675 from the company's Benton Harbor plant in Michigan. The two loaders, along with all of the remaining spare parts, were

Caterpillar 992G

Caterpillar officially introduced its innovative 992G wheel loader at the September 1996 MINExpo in Las Vegas, Nevada, intended as the eventual replacement for the 710 fhp Cat 992D model. The most distinguishing feature on the 992G is its one-piece, cast-steel, box-section front lift arm design, instead of the former twin-boom configuration. The loader is powered by a Cat 3508B EUI diesel engine, developing 880 gross hp and 800 fhp. The standard bucket capacity is 16 cubic yards. The length of the 992G is 53 feet, with an overall working weight of 201,982 pounds. The 992G was officially released for sale in March 1997. *Caterpillar*

Caterpillar 994
This Cat 994, pictured in October 1995, was the first unit equipped with the optional large-volume 45-cubic -yard coal-loading bucket. It makes its home at Powder River Coal's Rawhide Mine, located in the Powder River Basin of Wyoming. The standard bucket capacity for the Caterpillar 994 is 23 cubic yards, with a maximum 70,000-pound load limit. The 994 has an average length of 54 feet, 7 inches and an operating weight of 404,000 pounds. *ECO*

R. G. LeTourneau
Developer of the electric motorized wheel concept for heavy earth-moving applications, R. G. LeTourneau is shown with some of his diesel-electric drive creations in 1961. Starting with Mr. LeTourneau, continuing clockwise and ending dead center, are the M50-55 Power Packer, K-53F Pacemaker, K-103 Pacemaker, L-140 Electric Digger, LTU Electric Digger, K-205 Pacemaker, SL-10 Short Lever Shovel, L-60 Electric Digger, L-28 Electric Digger, L-27 Electric Digger, K-104 Pacemaker, K-54 Pacemaker, and the LTU-27 Electric Digger. *LeTourneau University*

R. G. LeTourneau SL-40

The largest conventional wheel loader built by R. G. LeTourneau that utilized a rack-and-pinion system was the SL-40. The SL-40 was powered by two rear-mounted GM Detroit Diesel 12V-71N engines, rated at 950 gross hp and 882 fhp. The standard bucket capacity for the big loader was rated at 19 cubic yards, with a maximum 40-ton payload. The SL-40 was 52 feet, 8 inches in length and weighed 147,000 pounds. Pictured at the Longview, Texas, plant in 1964 is the prototype SL-40. The modified preproduction version started testing in March 1965, and the unit was officially introduced at the October 1965 American Mining Congress (AMC) show in Las Vegas, Nevada. *ECO Collection*

R. G. LeTourneau XL-1 (L-700) Letric-Loader

R. G. LeTourneau was reluctant to give up on the electric-driven rack-and-pinion systems he had been using on his loader creations. But even he realized the benefits hydraulic cylinder technology would bring to the company's wheel loader designs. Pictured in March 1968 is the company's first electric-drive wheel loader to utilize hydraulic controls, the XL-1 Letric-Loader. The XL-1 was, in fact, the prototype for the model L-700. After further refinement of the prototype, including the relocation of the air cleaners, a preproduction L-700 was introduced in February 1969. The L-700 was powered by a GM Detroit Diesel 16V-71T-N75 engine, rated at 700 fhp. The bucket capacity was rated at 15 cubic yards, with a maximum 45,000-pound load limit. The working weight was 175,000 pounds. *ECO Collection*

shipped in 1988 to NERCO's Spring Creek Coal Mine in Montana. After this, the book was closed on the 675 loader program.

The Michigan loader program seemed to demonstrate the flaws of the twin-engine design, but that did not keep the Surface Mining Equipment for Coal Technology Research Association (SMEC) of Japan from developing a wheel loader that was very close in concept to that of the old 675 machine. Established in March 1983, SMEC was organized by 11 Japanese construction equipment manufacturers under the guidance of the Ministry of International Trade and Industry. The association's purpose was to develop large mining equipment to help in the exploration and acquisition of potential energy sources, namely coal. At the time, no Japanese manufacturer was willing to take on the enormous financial risk of developing a giant wheel loader on its own. But if the costs could be spread out over many builders and suppliers, the project became more attractive.

In 1986, the association released its first major product, the SMEC 180t super wheel loader. Built primarily by Kawasaki Heavy Industries, Ltd., of Japan, the SMEC was powered by two Cummins diesel engines with a combined power output of 1,341 fhp. The standard bucket capacity was 25 cubic yards, with a whopping 77,000-pound load rating. The tires were the same 67-inch size found on the Michigan 675C, but now they were made by Bridgestone, as Goodyear had discontinued that particular size. The first SMEC 180t unit started testing in 1987 at a quarry owned by Okumura Gumi Civil Engineering Co., Ltd., on Nishijima Island. From there it was shipped to Australia for further testing. In its field trials, the loader performed up to expectations, but the mining industry as a whole was simply not interested in another twin-engined wheel loader. The mild recession of the early 1990s, plus the advances in large wheel loader development coming from other non-Japanese companies, convinced the SMEC organization it should disband. Still, its experimental SMEC 180t did take the title of the world's largest wheel loader away from the Clark Michigan 675C, if only by a slim margin.

During the introduction of the SMEC super wheel loader in Japan, another Japanese company, Komatsu, was preparing to release the first of its large loaders, the WA800-1. Though not in the same size class as the giant SMEC design, the Komatsu WA800-1 was a wheel loader of ample proportions. Introduced in 1986, the 13.7-cubic yard capacity loader was aimed directly at customers interested in the

Caterpillar 992C model. The WA800-1 actually had more power than the big Cat, with ratings of 833 gross hp and 789 fhp. In 1988, Komatsu released the WA800-2 model, which offered better performance and reliability, and 10 years later the WA800-3 with a larger 14.4-cubic yard bucket, and 808 fhp. This model was released in Japan and Australia first, followed by the North American market in 1999.

In 1996, Komatsu introduced an even more powerful wheel loader than the WA800-2 in the form of the WA900-1. The WA900-1 shares much of its chassis with its sister machine, but has a higher power output, rated at 897 gross hp and 853 fhp, and carries a larger, 17-cubic yard bucket. The overall outside dimensions and weights of the two models are almost identical, with the WA900-1 weighing a bit more than the WA800-2.

When Komatsu discontinued the Haulpak 4000 model line back in 1995, it was left without a competitor in the large mining wheel loader market. But that is about to change. In 1998 Komatsu introduced a large, 26-cubic yard capacity, mechanical-drive wheel loader, identified as the WA1200-1, into its long-term engineering field testing program. This model promises to put Komatsu into direct competition with the world's other two large loader manufacturers, Caterpillar and LeTourneau.

Caterpillar unveiled its massive 994 mechanical-drive wheel loader in October 1990. Words like "big" and "large" don't even begin to describe the size of this Cat. The 994 carries a standard 23-cubic yard rock bucket with a 70,000-pound capacity. Power output from the single Cat Diesel V-16 engine is 1,336 gross hp and 1,250 fhp. In the early months of operation, it became clear that the 994's tires would need to be improved. Its 49.5-57,68PR-size tires were actually nothing more than slightly modified and reinforced off-highway truck tires. Again, that was all the tire manufacturers had to offer at the time. Within a short time, however, new 53.5/85-57 and 55.5/80-57-size tires were made available, and they greatly increased the loader's all-around operating availability and productivity. In early 1999, an improved 994D model was introduced featuring the more efficient Cat 3516B diesel engine that produced 1,375 gross-hp and 1,250 fhp. The working weight of the big loader was up to 421,600 pounds.

Diesel-Electric Drive Loaders

Like those of the large mining truck industry, customers in the large wheel loader industry can choose between mechanical

Marathon LeTourneau L-1200 Letro-Loader
When the diesel-electric drive Marathon LeTourneau L-1200 was introduced in 1978, there was a perceived need for this size and type of loading system in the mining industry. The L-1200 weighed in at 335,000 pounds; only the Clark Michigan 675 loader weighed more at the time. The L-1200 was equipped with a 22-cubic yard bucket rated at 66,000 pounds capacity. Power came from either a GM Detroit Diesel 12V-149TI or a Cummins KTA2300, each producing 1,200 fhp. Despite its size and capability, the recession of the early 1980s dealt a death blow to the L-1200. In the end, only 11 loaders were built. Even today, the L-1200 with its 53-foot, 8-inch length is still considered a very, very big loader. Pictured working in June 1981 at Boliden Minerals' Copper Mine near Gallivare, Sweden, is an L-1200 equipped with the optional mammoth Goodyear 67-51,44PR(L-5)-series tires, the largest in the world. *ECO Collection*

LeTourneau L-1100 Letro-Loader
At the 1986 American Mining Congress show, LeTourneau unveiled its popular L-1100 Letro-Loader. Like all LeTourneau loaders, the L-1100 has diesel-electric drive. Though the 22-cubic yard capacity of the L-1100 is the same as that of the previous L-1200, the new loader can do more with less. Either a 12-cylinder Detroit Diesel 12V-149TI DDECIII or a Cummins KTA-38-C engine can be specified, each with a power rating of 1,050 fhp. The total operating weight of the machine is 276,000 pounds, and it is 50 feet, 4 inches in length. Shown in 1996 at Peabody Coal's Lee Ranch Mine near Grants, New Mexico, a L-1100 loads a WABCO coal hauler. *ECO*

and diesel-electric drive models. But there is only one manufacturer of diesel-electric wheel loaders—LeTourneau, Inc., of Longview, Texas. This is not surprising, since the concept of an electric traction wheel motor for earth-moving machinery applications was born in this company. After R. G. LeTourneau had sold the earth-moving vehicle manufacturing part of his business to Westinghouse Air Brake Company in 1953, he invested a good part of the proceeds in the development of the electric wheel concept, which was utilized in many of his creations outside the earth-moving industry. After a five-year moratorium on competing directly with LeTourneau-Westinghouse ended in 1958, Mr. LeTourneau unleashed a tidal wave of new earth-moving equipment designs based on the diesel-electric drive system utilizing traction wheel motors. Wheel loader models quickly followed his first scraper introductions. One of the first models to be tested was the SL-10 Short Lever Shovel in 1960. The SL-10 was a three-wheel design, equipped with a 10-cubic yard bucket. Though looking nothing like the wheel loaders we are accustomed to today, it was nonetheless a starting point for LeTourneau. More conventional-looking prototypes of articulated-frame steering models were soon to follow. In 1964, LeTourneau

introduced the 15-cubic yard model SL-30, and in the latter part of that year, the prototype 19-cubic yard SL-40. These were followed by the smaller 7.5-cubic yard SL-15, and 10-cubic yard SL-20, both in 1965.

All of these creations relied on the use of electric-driven, rack-and-pinion gear assemblies to raise and lower the boom, steer, and dump the bucket. However, to compete effectively in the wheel loader market, hydraulic systems were needed to control all of these functions. Mr. LeTourneau was never interested in hydraulic controls, feeling that they were too inefficient when compared to electric motors. Under pressure from competitors, LeTourneau finally agreed with his engineers to adopt hydraulics and mothball the archaic electric rack-and-pinion systems. In March 1968, the company unveiled its first experimental wheel loader equipped with hydraulic controls, the XL-1 "Letric-Loader." Modern in design, large in capacity, and driven by electric wheel motors at all four corners, it would form the basis for all LeTourneau wheel loader models yet to come. After further engineering work on the prototype, the loader received the model designation L-700. In February 1969, the 15-cubic yard prototype L-700, now referred to as a "Letro-Loader," was finally ready to start long-term field testing.

Following in the XL-1's footsteps was a smaller 10-cubic yard loader called the XL-2, which was unveiled in February 1969 as the L-500. Designed in 1968 as a further expansion of the new loader product line, the L-500 series was put on hold indefinitely in 1969, when the company ran into financial difficulties. LeTourneau could afford to fund only one wheel loader design platform, and they chose the larger L-700, anticipating greater sales. Only one XL-2/L-500 loader was ever built.

After the death of R. G. LeTourneau on June 1, 1969, the company was eventually sold to Marathon Manufacturing Company in September 1970. At first the company remained R. G. LeTourneau, Inc., and operated as a subsidiary of Marathon Manufacturing. By 1974, the company was simply referred to as Marathon LeTourneau.

In total, 76 units of the L-700, including the prototype, were built by the time the model was upgraded into the L-800 series in 1975. In fact, the prototype L-800 loader was built out of the L-700 prototype unit. The L-800 carried the same-size bucket as the L-700, but the new model was more powerful, with 860 gross hp available from its Detroit Diesel engine, or 800 gross hp from an available Cummins unit. During its production run from 1975 to 1983,

Western 2000

The diesel-electric drive Western 2000 wheeled push-dozer was designed to push-load scrapers at speeds that far exceeded tracked dozers. The 2000 was conceived of by Western Contracting Corporation, owner of the Western 80 hauler. A 16-cylinder, GM 16-278A diesel marine engine supplied power to GE electric traction motors installed in the ends of each axle. The electric motors were connected to the wheels' planetary gear housings in the hubs by shafts from the motors. The total output was 2,000 gross hp and 1,650

fhp, with an auxiliary 200-gross hp GM diesel powering an AC generator. The pusher was 47 feet long and weighed in at 340,000 pounds. Special Goodyear 44.5-45,38PR-size tires were employed on the big push-dozer; they were 10 feet in diameter, the largest available at the time. Introduced in 1963, its first assignment was at the Milford Dam project in Kansas. Pictured on location in 1964, it is shown push-loading a Euclid SS-40 Scraper. Only one Western 2000 was ever built. *Western Contracting Corp.*

Marathon LeTourneau built 193 L-800 machines, not counting the reengineered L-700/L-800 prototype. The L-800 model line was a clear success story for the company.

In mid-1977, the company tried again to introduce a 10-cubic yard loader in the form of the L-600. This 525-fhp wheel loader might have had a better chance of success had it not been for the fact that the upgraded Caterpillar 992C was released the same year. The 992C was more than a match for the L-600; only 26 L-600 loaders were ever built.

Next to join the electric-drive loader line was the giant L-1200 loader, which was first seen in prototype form at the October 1978 American Mining Congress (AMC) show in Las Vegas, Nevada. The L-1200 carried a 22-cubic yard bucket with a 66,000-pound load rating and a 1200-fhp diesel engine. Unfortunately for Marathon LeTourneau, by the time production units were available on the L-1200, the worldwide economic recession was under way, and the L-1200 would not survive it. In all, three prototype and eight production machines were built, with the last six units delivered to a coal mining operation in Colombia, South America.

Marathon LeTourneau's replacement for the L-800 model line was the larger, 17-cubic yard, 51,000-pound-capacity L-1000. The first 900-fhp prototype unit was shipped from the Longview, Texas, plant in September 1982, and the first production loader in July 1983. The L-1000 was

LeTourneau L-1400 Letro-Loader

In November 1990, LeTourneau put its first massive L-1400 wheel loader to work. No other machine up to that point had ever carried a standard 28-cubic yard rock bucket with an 84,000-pound load capacity. The power ratings for the L-1400 are 1,800 fhp, available from either a 16-cylinder Detroit Diesel 16V-149TI DDECIII or Cummins K-1800E diesel engine. The L-1400 weighs in at a stout 445,000 pounds. The length of the loader is 56 feet, 6 inches. Pictured working in 1995 at Dry Fork Coal in the Powder River Basin near Gillette, Wyoming, is an L-1400 equipped with an optional 43-cubic yard combo-bucket for coal-loading applications. *ECO*

LeTourneau L-1800 Letro-Loader

In December 1993, LeTourneau took the wraps off its newest electric-drive wheel loader, the giant L-1800 Letro-Loader. First announced at the 1992 American Mining Congress show in Las Vegas, Nevada, the L-1800 is the largest wheel loader ever built. Equipped with a standard 33-cubic yard rock bucket with a 100,000-pound load rating, it can do the jobs that were once reserved only for cable and hydraulic mining shovels. The engine choices are a Detroit Diesel 16V-149TI DDECIII or a Cummins K-1800E unit. Both power plants are 16-cylinder engines rated at 1,800 fhp, with optional 2,000-fhp configurations available—more than enough power to hustle this big 480,000-pound loader around without difficulty. LeTourneau shipped the first L-1800 unit in July 1994. It is pictured here equipped with a 45-cubic yard combo-bucket, working at AMAX Coal's Eagle Butte Mine near Gillette, Wyoming. *ECO*

R. G. LeTourneau Series K-205 Pacemaker
Of all of the early diesel-electric drive Pacemaker tractors built by R. G. LeTourneau, the Series K-205 was by far the largest and most powerful. Introduced in March 1961, the K-205 was powered by three rear-mounted Cummins V-12 diesel engines, rated at 1,260 gross hp combined. All five wheels were driven by internal electric traction motors. With a 20-foot blade and a 50-foot, 3-inch length, the K-205 was considered a very large tractor-dozer. The average operating weight of the unit was 320,000 pounds. *ECO Collection*

R. G. LeTourneau K-600A
The T-600 series, originally known as the K-600A, employed an old-style rack-and-pinion control of the blade. It was one of the largest articulated, electric-drive tractors of this type built by R. G. LeTourneau. The original K-600A was introduced in August 1967 as a pusher unit for scraper loading applications. The K-600A was powered by a GM Detroit Diesel 16V-71N engine, rated at 635 gross hp and 609 fhp. The tractor had an electric-traction motor in each wheel, giving the unit four-wheel drive, and was steered by means of an articulated chassis. A 16-foot-wide dozing blade was also available instead of the push-block. The working weight of the unit was 136,440 pounds. An upgraded T-600B model was announced in 1969. *ECO Collection*

considered a success for the company, and is still offered in its product line.

At the fall AMC show in 1986, Marathon LeTourneau unveiled the company's latest entry in the 22-cubic yard capacity class of loaders, the L-1100. Even though the capacity ratings were the same as the discontinued L-1200, the loader was an entirely new design. In December 1986, the first 1,050-fhp prototype was shipped to its new home at a coal mine in Kentucky.

In November 1990, Marathon Le-Tourneau introduced its big L-1400 loader. Carrying a standard 28-cubic yard rock bucket capable of handling an 84,000-pound payload, the L-1400 became the largest wheel loader in the world. Either a Cummins or a Detroit Diesel engine could be specified, both rated at 1,600 fhp. By 1996, power output had risen to 1,800 fhp.

At the 1992 AMC show, Marathon Le-Tourneau released preliminary specifications of a wheel loader that was even larger than its L-1400. Identified as the L-1800, the first unit was officially unveiled at the Longview plant in December 1993. It was equipped with a standard 33-cubic yard-bucket that could handle an incredible 100,000-pound payload. With its introduction, the title of the world's largest wheel loader transferred from

Marathon LeTourneau D-800 Letro-Dozer
Developed from the L-800 Letro-Loader, the Marathon LeTourneau D-800 diesel-electric drive Letro-dozer was introduced in October 1978; it was intended for use in land reclamation projects and for coal stockpiling. Power was supplied to the electric wheel motors by either a 12-cylinder Cummins KT-2300-C diesel engine, rated at 900 gross hp and 820 fhp, or a 16- cylinder Detroit Diesel 16V-92T, with 860 gross hp and 800 fhp. Two blades were offered—a coal blade 22 feet, 5 inches wide, or a reclamation version (pictured) that was 21 feet, 3 inches wide. The maximum operating weight was 194,400 pounds. *LeTourneau*

the L-1400 to the L-1800. The loader was powered by an 1,800-fhp standard engine, with 2,000-fhp engine options-available.

In February 1994, Rowan Companies, Inc., purchased the Marathon LeTourneau Company. Rowan had been one of the largest customers for Marathon Le-Tourneau's oil drilling rig platforms, and wanted to make sure that LeTourneau would be there when they needed them. So they bought the company. The Marathon part of the name was dropped, and the company reinstated its older "L" logo design, with the new name of LeTourneau, Inc., a tribute to R. G. LeTourneau, who originally developed the close working ties between the company and Rowan.

In October 1998, LeTourneau was able to increase the loading capacity of its L-

1800 wheel loader, when it delivered the industry's first 55-cubic yard coal loading bucket for use at Powder River Coal's Rochelle North Antelope Complex, in the Powder River Basin of Wyoming. Only a few years before, this was considered a good-size coal loading bucket for a mining cable-shovel.

In September 1998, LeTourneau announced it's latest electric-drive wheel loader—the 26-cubic yard capacity L-1350. The first prototype machine started testing at the Longview plant in March 1999. The 1500-fhp LeTourneau L-1350 model joins the more than 570 Letro-Loaders that have been built since the end of 1998.

Almost a footnote in the history of electric-drive wheel loaders was the at-

tempt by Dart in 1974 to introduce a competing model to Marathon LeTourneau's L-700A. Dart produced two loader proposals, the DE620 and DE900. The DE620 was a 700-gross-hp-rated loader equipped with a 15-cubic yard, 45,000-pound, capacity bucket. The DE900 was a much larger design, with a 1,325-gross-hp Detroit Diesel engine, and a 21-cubic yard bucket with a 63,000-pound rating. Both of these designs had diesel-electric drivetrains, but the DE620 system utilized a single electric traction motor connected to each axle housing. The proposed system in the DE900 placed a traction wheel motor in the hub assembly of each driving wheel, much like the Le-Tourneau layout. But in the end, Dart only produced 12 of the DE620 loaders, and none of the larger DE900 models.

VCON V-250

VCON, an acronym for Vehicle Constructors, was a division of the Peerless Manufacturing Company, located in Dallas, Texas. In 1969 the company announced the development of a large tractor called the V-250 Pusher. This machine was designed to push scrapers when it was first delivered to a uranium mine in June 1970. After the first 1,000 hours of operation, the push-block was removed and replaced with a 22-foot wide bulldozer blade in 1972. The V-250 was powered by a 1,000-gross hp diesel engine. The length was 40 feet, 8 inches, and the full operating weight was 250,000 pounds. The only prototype V-250 unit ever built is pictured here working in July 1974, just before being shipped to Canada to undergo further testing in the oil tar sands of northern Alberta. *ECO Collection*

Clark Michigan Model 480

After a year of prototype testing, in 1958 Clark Michigan offered its big Model 480 tractor-dozer as an efficient means of loading scrapers. The 480 was powered by a Cummins VT-12 diesel engine, rated at 600 gross hp. Later models also offered the GM Detroit Diesel 16V-71N with 635 gross hp. The wheel tractor could be equipped with a dozing blade 14 feet wide, or with a Michigan "Pushin'-Cushin" block for push-loading scrapers. The 480 Series III shown, first released in 1965, is equipped with the GM engine and push-block. The working weight of the tractor was 105,000 pounds. A total of only 90 units had been built by the time the last tractor left the factory in 1966. *ECO Collection*

Wheel Dozers

Today's rubber-tire wheel dozer combines the best elements of two popular pieces of earth-moving equipment, the bulldozer and the articulated wheel loader. By utilizing the articulated chassis of the wheel loader in combination with a dozer blade, it is possible to produce a highly versatile machine.

One of the first practical wheel dozers produced in the earth-moving industry was the Tournadozer, built by R. G. LeTourneau in September 1946. The Tournadozer was a small, speedy tractor with rubber tires that steered by means of an air-actuated steering clutch. The clutches were used during braking to engage and disengage the left- or right-side driving wheels. Articulated frame steering was still some years off at this time.

Production officially started in January 1947 with the Tournadozer Model C1. Largest of the Tournadozers was the experimental Model A tractor, first built in September 1947. At the Chicago Road Show in 1948, LeTourneau displayed a Tournadozer Super Model A, powered by a 750-gross-hp Packard marine engine. Overpowered by its own engine, the Model A was difficult to handle, and was eventually removed from any further testing by 1950.

After R. G. LeTourneau reentered the earth-moving industry in 1958, he soon began to fabricate large, electric-drive wheel dozers. These creations paralleled his scraper and wheel loader programs, which all utilized his electric traction wheel motors. The largest of these early designs was the Pacemaker Series K-205 Tractor. The K-205 utilized five electric-drive wheels, powered by three 420-gross-hp Cummins V-12 diesel engines with a combined 1,260-gross-hp rating, and it carried a dozing push blade that was 20 feet wide.

The industry was not very receptive to these "wild" creations of LeTourneau, so back to the drawing board he went, to come up with something that was a bit more conventional. In September 1965, the R. G. LeTourneau K-54 Dozer started testing. This K-54 model had diesel electric-drive system, but what distinguished it was the use of an articulated frame for steering. This tractor was eventually released as the 475 gross-hp T-450-A in 1966. Other models to follow included the 318 gross-hp T-300-A in 1966, and the 635 gross-hp K-600-A (later identified as the T-600-A) in August 1967. The last of the wheel dozers to have the involvement of R. G. LeTourneau was the XT-1 project, which became the D-450-B when it was unveiled in February 1969. This 530-gross-hp and 475-fhp wheel dozer was based on the L-500 loader, which was designed at the same time as the dozer unit and was equipped with hydraulic control systems for all blade functions. But the same financial problems that sunk the L-500 loader took the D-450-B tractor dozer as well. Only one unit was ever produced.

Marathon LeTourneau was to give the diesel-electric drive wheel dozer one more try when it introduced the D-800 Letro-Dozer at the October AMC show in 1978. Based on the L-800 loader platform, the D-800 was a thoroughly modern design that packed an 860-gross hp, 800-fhp diesel engine in the rear. But as with the L-1200 loader, the economic recession at the time doomed the big electric dozer. The L-800 was finally replaced in 1983 by the L-1000, and the D-800 was discontinued.

The LeTourneau wheel dozers were not the only type produced with electric drive systems. In 1963, Western Contracting Corporation introduced a one-of-a-kind tractor called the Western 2000, specially

International-Hough D-500 PAY Dozer
The Frank G. Hough Company, a subsidiary of International Harvester Co., introduced the industry's first large pivot-steer pusher-dozer—the Hough D-500 "PAY Dozer." The first prototype D-500 started testing in 1959, with the first production versions introduced in late 1961. The D-500 was powered by a Cummins VT-12-700-CI diesel engine, rated at 700 horsepower, but de-rated to 600 gross hp for long engine life. Later, a GM Detroit Diesel 16V-71N powerplant, rated at 635 gross hp, was made available. The D-500 could be equipped with a push-block for scraper loading applications, or with a dozer blade 13 feet, 5 inches wide. the overall working weight was 145,000 pounds. In 1964, Hough introduced its 10-cubic yard wheel loader, the H-400 PAY Loader, which was based on the D-500 wheel dozer program. *ECO Collection*

Caterpillar 854G
The Caterpillar 854G wheel dozer actually began as the Tiger 790G, developed by Tiger Engineering Pty., Ltd., of Australia and unveiled at the September 1996 MINExpo in Las Vegas, Nevada. In late 1997, Caterpillar purchased the rights to all of the company's wheel dozers and, in May 1998, officially introduced the Tiger 790G as the Cat 854G. The 854G rear chassis and drivetrain is based on the Caterpillar 992G wheel loader, and a two-plate front frame and heavy-duty blade linkage from the D11R dozer completes the package. The 854G is powered by a Cat 3508B EUI diesel engine, rated at 880 gross hp and 800 fhp. A semi U-blade rated at 33 cubic yards and 20 feet, 7 inches in width, or a coal blade rated at 58.2 cubic yards that is 23 feet, 7 inches in width are available. The maximum working weight of the big Cat is 213,632 pounds. *Caterpillar*

designed for them by C.W. Jones Engineering Co. of Los Angeles—the same firm that designed the massive Western 80 hauler. The unit was actually built by Intercontinental Engineering-Manufacturing Corp. of Parkville, Missouri, in 10 months. Designed as a push-tractor for scraper loading applications, the Western 2000 was powered by a massive GM diesel marine engine rated at 2,000 gross hp and 1,650 fhp. Even today, the Western 2000 is still considered the largest push-dozer ever put into service. Only one of these monsters was ever built, and it was finally scrapped in 1981.

Over the years, big conventional diesel-powered wheel dozers have been widely accepted in the earth-moving industry. But of the many companies that produced these machines, only a few built very large ones. These include the Clark Michigan Model 480, from 1958; the Hough D-500 PAY Dozer, from 1961; the Allis-Chalmers 555, from 1963; the RayGo Grizzly 150, from 1971; the Melroe M880 Multi-Wheel Dozer, from 1976; and the FWD-Wagner WI-30 pusher-dozer, from the mid-1960s.

In 1970, Peerless Manufacturing Company, builder of the VCON 3006 mining hauler, introduced its first prototype diesel-electric drive wheel tractor—the VCON V-250. Even though the V-250 worked at various mining locations throughout North America, its main purpose was as a test bed for an even larger wheel dozer called the V-220. After Marion Power Shovel had

VCON V-220

In June 1975, Marion introduced the world's largest wheel dozer, the VCON V-220. Power came from a Detroit Diesel 16V-149T engine driving four GE electric motors, one in each wheel. The total output was 1,500 gross hp and 1,320 fhp. Many publications over the years have listed the power rating of this machine as high as 2,600 horsepower. This rating was for an optional engine, and neither of the two production dozers ever used it. The V-220 was equipped with an enormous 26-foot-wide, semi-U blade. The overall length was 51 feet, 8 inches. The total weight was 150 tons—275,000 pounds for the tractor and 25,000 pounds for the blade. Only two V-220s and one prototype V-250 were manufactured. An option of a 35-cubic yard load and carry bucket was offered, but none were ever produced. Also, plans were drawn up to produce a VCON wheel loader, but only a small-scale engineering model ever saw the light of day. *ECO Collection*

Tiger 690D
One of the most popular wheel dozers to be built by Tiger Engineering Pty., Ltd., of Australia was its 690D model, first released in 1993. The Tiger 690D was based on Caterpillar's 992D wheel loader, with the hydraulic blade system from the Cat D10N. Power was supplied by a Cat 3412C diesel engine, rated at 755 gross hp and 710 fhp. With its single joystick "STIC Control System," all maneuvering of the dozer is controlled with one hand, reducing shoulder and back fatigue. This feature makes the Tiger one of the more desirable machines to operate on the job. The 690D weighs in at 197,900 pounds. *ECO*

purchased the Vehicle Constructors (VCON) division from Peerless in June 1974, work started in earnest on the V-220 project. In June 1975, the first gigantic V-220 was a reality. With 1,500 gross hp and 1,320 fhp behind its electric-drive system, the VCON had the muscle to handle its 26-foot-wide blade. Weighing in at 150 tons, the V-220 was the world's largest wheel dozer. The VCON dozers showed promise of great performance, especially in land reclamation dozing, but potential customers were wary of such a specialized piece of equipment. After Dresser Industries bought Marion in 1977, the VCON dozers were put on the back burner. Soon they were forgotten altogether.

Of all the builders of large wheel dozers, Tiger Engineering Pty. Ltd., of Western Australia, has probably had the most success at

marketing these machines to the mining industry. Established in 1980, Tiger built its first mechanical-drive wheel dozer, the 690A, in 1981. The Tiger 690A was based largely on the Caterpillar 992C wheel loader equipped with a Tiger-designed front frame section. In 1985, an improved 690B model was introduced. The model was upgraded again in 1993 into the 690D, which had followed the design lead of the Cat 992D wheel loader. With its joystick control, the Tiger 690D was a favorite among operators. The last of the big Tigers to be introduced was the 790G in September 1996. Based on the Cat 992G loader, it was the most powerful Tiger to be built.

With sales on the rise and the future looking bright for Tiger, Caterpillar decided to expand its wheel dozer product line in the autumn of 1997 by acquiring

the intellectual property rights to design and manufacture the wheel dozers from Tiger. Caterpillar and Tiger had always enjoyed a close working relationship, since Tiger's wheeldozers were sold and serviced through the Caterpillar dealer network worldwide. In May 1998, Caterpillar officially added the two Tiger machines to its wheel dozer product line—as the Cat 854G and 844 models. The Cat 854G was the former Tiger 790G, and the 844's alter ego was the Tiger 590B. Both of these models join Cat's other wheel dozer offerings, which include the long-running 834B model. Introduced in 1963 as the 834, it has been the most popular wheel dozer choice in the mining industry. If the 834 series is any indication, it seems we will be seeing a lot more of these new Caterpillars in the years to come.

6 SCRAPERS AND GRADERS

The origins of large, self-propelled, rubber-tire scrapers can be traced directly back to one individual— Robert Gilmour LeTourneau. Though LeTourneau was involved in all areas of earth-moving equipment building, scrapers really put him and his company on the map. R. G. LeTourneau built his first "drag-type" scraper in 1922. Later in that same year, he built a second scraper model called the Gondola. Unique to this small 6-cubic yard unit was its brazed metal construction—an innovation in the industry. Before this, all parts were held together by metal rivets. In 1923, he built his third scraper, the 12-cubic -yard "Mountain Mover." With its two-bucket bowl design, the scraper was able to fill faster, increasing productivity dramatically. Also in late 1923, LeTourneau designed and built the first self-propelled scraper, which was mounted on steel wheels and controlled by DC electric power motors. In 1929, R. G. LeTourneau, Inc., was officially formed in California, and in 1932, the company released its first 9-cubic yard Model A Carryall scraper.

But the real industry-changing model introduction occurred in March 1938 with the building of the world's first self-propelled, rubber-tire scraper, called the Model A "Tournapull." This first Tournapull pulled its experimental prototype Z25 Carryall scraper unit by means of a single-axle tractor, powered by a Caterpillar diesel engine. This one model, more than any other, would shape the look of high-speed, self-propelled scrapers for years to come.

When LeTourneau sold the rights to his earth-moving equipment business to the Westinghouse Air Brake Co. in 1953, the new company of LeTourneau-Westing-house continued on with the production of Tournapull and Carryall scrapers. Meanwhile, R. G. LeTourneau continued building forestry and logging equipment, as well as off-shore oil drilling platforms. R. G. LeTourneau was allowed to start marketing earth-moving equipment again in 1958, and he did so immediately, introducing numerous diesel-electric powered earth-moving machines using his electric-wheel concept. The first of the earth-moving machines to be introduced was the Model A-4 "Goliath" at the American Mining Congress show in San Francisco, California, in September 1958. Goliath was a 600-gross -hp diesel-electric drive scraper, capable of carrying 50 to 60 cubic yards of earth and with a payload of more than 70 tons. At 62 feet in length, it was considered a monster for its day. But even bigger and more powerful scraper creations that would make Goliath seem small by comparison were soon to surface from LeTourneau.

Starting in October 1958, a number of earth-moving machines were released in succession by the company under the trade name, "Electric Digger." The first of these was the tandem-bowled Pacemaker L-130, followed by the L-140, in late 1960; the L-60, in 1961; and the L-70 and L-90, in 1964, to name just a few. But one unit stands out from all of the rest. It is the Pacemaker Series LT-360 Electric-Digger, the world's largest self-propelled scraper.

The history of the LT-360 started in March 1965 with the introduction of the LT-120. This 72-cubic -yard scraper was powered by four diesel engines, producing 2,220 gross hp and 2,100 fhp. In April 1965, an additional scraper unit was added to the LT-120, turning it into the LT-240.

R. G. LeTourneau Series LT-300

The R. G. LeTourneau Series LT-300 Electric-Digger made its first appearance in August 1966. This experimental model consisted of a scraper front unit with an attached bulldozing blade powered by four Detroit Diesel 16V-71 engines. The rear scraper portion, which was borrowed from the redesigned prototype Series LT-360, was powered by three 16V-71 powerplants. Combined, these engines produced 4,445 gross hp and 4,263 fhp. All six wheels were driven by internal electric traction wheel-motors. The capacity in the front scraper was 100 cubic yards and 72 cubic yards for the rear unit. The total payload capacity was 300 tons. The overall length was 148 feet. *LeTourneau*

The LT-240 was powered by five diesel engines, producing 2,855 gross hp and 2,709 fhp. The capacity was rated at 144 cubic yards. Another scraper unit was added in August 1965, and the model name was changed to the LT-360. The diesel-electric drive LT-360 was powered by eight Detroit Diesel engines—six 16V-71 engines and two 12V-71 engines—totaling 4,760 gross hp and 4,536 fhp and driving 12 wheels. The capacity was a whopping 216 cubic yards, rated at 360 tons. After the LT-360 went through some proving ground testing at the LeTourneau Longview plant, the unit was briefly put into service during August 1965 working on part of the Interstate 20 project in East Texas. There it joined other large LeTourneau equipment that had been working at the site since July. The LT-360 only worked a few months of the project, which was finished in December.

After the LT-360 was shipped back to the Longview plant, a series of design modifications were made to the LT-360 to

R. G. LeTourneau Tournapull Model A6

Of the early mechanical, self-propelled wheel-scrapers built by R. G. LeTourneau, the Model A6 Tournapull, equipped with an OU Carryall scraper, was the largest. The A6 Tournapull and OU Carryall started development in 1941 with the OU Carryall introduced first, in January 1942. The test tractor for the OU scraper was the A6 Tournapull's predecessor, the twin-engined A5. The Model A6 was officially unveiled in April 1942. The clutch-steered A6 was powered by two supercharged Cummins HBISD-600 diesel engines rated at 400 gross hp total, mounted side by side and coupled to a LeTourneau-designed power-shift automatic transmission. The double-bucket OU scraper was rated at 45 cubic yards struck and 60 heaped, which was considered massive for the time. But due to the military production needs of World War II, further development of the model line was suspended. *ECO Collection*

R. G. LeTourneau Model A-4
Series L-70 *Goliath*

Before R. G. LeTourneau introduced the electric-drive wheel concept for large wheel loaders, it was first utilized in earth-moving applications in the massive diesel-electric drive scrapers from the late 1950s and early 1960s. After his noncompete agreement expired on May 1, 1958, LeTourneau was allowed to reenter the earth-moving market. At the September 1958 American Mining Congress show, held in San Francisco, California, he unveiled his first diesel-electric drive scraper design—the Model A-4 Series L-70 *Goliath*. Powered by a 600-gross-hp Cummins diesel engine, it was capable of handling a 50- to 60-cubic yard capacity with a maximum 70-ton payload limit. It was surpassed in size in October 1958 when LeTourneau introduced its tandem-bowled Series L-130 Electric-Digger. *ECO Collection*

R. G. LeTourneau Series L-90

The most successful of the large, multibowled, electric-drive scrapers built by R. G. LeTourneau was the Series L-90 Electric-Digger. Introduced in May 1964, it was derived from the triple-bowled scraper unit Series L-70, from February 1964. The L-90 was powered by three Detroit Diesel 12V-71N engines, developing 1,425 gross hp and 1,323 fhp—the same engines as that found in the 12-wheel L-70. The capacity for the L-90 was 57 cubic yards struck and 72 heaped, with a 90-ton load limit. The L-90 was available with electric-drive wheel combinations of 7, 8, or 12 wheels. The overall length of the 12-wheel model was almost 108 feet. The empty working weight was 253,000 pounds. This 12-wheel L-90 is pictured in October 1967 working in Fort Myers, Florida. *ECO Collection*

R. G. LeTourneau Series LT-240

The R. G. LeTourneau Series LT-240 Electric-Digger was introduced in April 1965. The LT-240 included the original LT-120 from March 1965, minus an engine, plus an additional powered scraper unit. The LT-240 was powered by five diesel engines—two Detroit Diesel 12V-71N engines located in the front power module, and three 16V-71N units mounted on the scrapers. The total output for all five engines was 2,855 gross hp and 2,709 fhp. All six wheels contained electric traction motors. The total capacity was 144 cubic yards with a maximum 240-ton payload. By August 1965, the LT-240 was modified and incorporated into the original 12-wheel drive, three-scraper bowl LT-360 Electric-Digger. *ECO Collection*

address performance problems encountered at the work site. The main drive wheels were reduced to eight in the hopes of reducing the overall turning radius of the unit—which was enormous. Also, all eight of the LT-360's engines were now Detroit Diesel 16V-71 engines, with a total rating of 5,080 gross hp and 4,872 fhp. The capacity remained unchanged. The redesigned LT-360 was ready in March 1966, but the unit would never have another chance to prove itself in this large configuration. The LT-360 was simply too big for its own good. The original design was just over 175 feet long, and the second design measured in at 200 feet in length; size in these proportions proved unmanageable at the worksite.

The last of the mammoth multi-unit Electric-Diggers to be introduced was the LT-300, which started testing in August 1966. The front unit of the scraper was rated at 100 cubic yards, while the rear portion carried 72 cubic yards. Seven Detroit Diesel 16V-71 engines pumped out 4,445 gross hp and 4,263 fhp, driving six wheels. The rear scraper on the LT-300 was, in fact, the third unit of the LT-360, with another engine grafted on. The part of the LT-360 that was left was now called the LT-240. But this time it was configured with six 16V-71 engines, producing 3,810 gross hp and 3,654 fhp. The capacity was the same as the original LT-240 from 1965. It can be somewhat confusing to look back on these machines and view them all as stand-alone models, when actually the LT-120, LT-240, LT-360, and

R. G. LeTourneau
Series LT-360

The LT-360 Electric-Digger, unveiled in August 1965, was the largest self-loading scraper LeTourneau had ever built. The company was never noted for the aesthetics of its designs, but rather for their absolute functionality. Here the LT-360 did not disappoint. The original LT-360 was built out of the prototype LT-240, with another scraper unit attached. It was powered by two Detroit Diesel 12V-71N engines and six 16V-71 engines, rated at 4,760 gross hp and 4,536 fhp combined. This original unit was driven by 12 internal wheel electric traction motors. In March 1966, the experimental LT-360 prototype, pictured, was shown again, this time with many design alterations. The scraper was powered by eight Detroit Diesel 16V-71 engines, producing an incredible 5,080 gross hp and 4,872 fhp. It also had 8 drive wheels instead of 12, which helped reduce its turning radius. The LT-360 could load its combined 216-cubic yard bowls with 360 tons of earth in 80 seconds. The overall length of the complete unit was 200 feet. *LeTourneau*

part of the LT-300 were all made out of each other. In the end, none of these experimental units ever found a permanent home, and they were all eventually scrapped to get them off the company's books.

While LeTourneau was building his enormous, multi-engine scrapers in the 1950s and 1960s, his original Tournapull and Carryall product lines were still being sold under the LeTourneau-Westinghouse (L-W) corporate name. L-W had been granted use of the LeTourneau name for marketing purposes under the terms of the sale. Though the arrangement created some confusion, Mr. LeTourneau had no part of this company, except as a consultant.

Some of the larger scrapers manufactured by L-W were the factory-produced tandem Model B Tournapulls with Model B Fullpak scraper units. The big tandem "B Pull," as it was called, was introduced in August 1960. It carried a full 50 cubic yards struck and 64 heaped, with a maximum 74-ton payload rating. In 1963, the designation of the scraper model line changed to the WABCO Model B-70 Tournapull.

Largest of L-W's conventional self-propelled tractor-pulled scrapers was its Model B Speedpull tandem and triple Fullpak units, which were first seen in January 1960. The Model B Speedpull was a 600-gross -hp, high-speed, two-axle tractor, pulling a set of tandem Model B Fullpak scraper units rated at 46 cubic yards struck and 58 heaped. When another Fullpak scraper was added to make it a triple combination, the capacity jumped to 69 cubic yards struck and 87 heaped, with a payload of 102 tons. The Model B Speedpull was also offered in a single scraper bowl configuration in 1961, matched up with the Model BM9 unit rated at 35 cubic yards struck and 45 heaped, with a maximum 52-ton payload. The big Speedpulls utilized the same type of electric-cable controls for scraper bowl functions as was found on all other Tournapull models. This was basically the same system introduced by R. G. LeTourneau back in 1946.

LeTourneau-Westinghouse/WABCO had experienced great success in the marketplace with its larger self-loading elevating scrapers. In 1963, WABCO introduced its Model B-70 with a 31-cubic yard Hancock 333 elevating scraper. By September

LeTourneau-Westinghouse Model B Speedpull Tandem Fullpak

The LeTourneau-Westinghouse Model B Speedpull, introduced in January 1960, was the big brother to the company's Model C Speedpull from 1959. The B Speedpull was available with single or tandem Model B Fullpak scraper units. The tractor was powered by a 600-gross-hp Turbo-Cummins VT-12 diesel engine. The B Tandem Fullpak scraper outfit was rated at 46 cubic yards struck and 58 heaped. The overall length of the tandem set was 76 feet, with an empty weight of 117,000 pounds. The B Speedpull became the WABCO Model 800 in 1963, which was available with a single Fullpak scraper unit rated at 36 cubic yards struck and 46 heaped. *ECO Collection*

1967, the company had introduced a 34-cubic yard, twin-engined version called the Model BT333F, which produced 950 gross hp and 885 fhp. In 1970, the designation for this model changed to the 333FT. By late 1977, the big WABCO 333FT was replaced by the even larger twin-engined Model 353FT. At 1,025 gross hp and 966 fhp, with a payload capacity of 36 cubic yards, it was the largest-production, self-loading, elevating scraper ever built—a distinction it holds to this day. Even though WABCO experimented with a Model 800 Speedpull tractor pulling tandem Hancock 444 elevating scrapers in June 1963, their combined capacity of 90 cubic yards was just a bit more than could be safely handled by the tractor and its operator. The unit never went into full production. By 1981, the last WABCO scraper built by the company was shipped, bringing the great story of the Tournapull—the industry's first rubber-tire, self-propelled scraper line—to an end.

Other large-capacity scrapers that competed against the L-W Tournapulls in the 1960s included the twin-engine Allis-Chalmers 562 introduced in 1962. Offered in a tandem-scraper configuration, the largest model was capable of handling a load of 66 cubic yards struck and 88 heaped. International Harvester also offered a twin-bowl IH 295 PAY Scraper, capable of a 48-cubic yard struck and 64 heaped payload. But one of the most powerful scrapers available at the time was the gigantic twin-engine, two-axle, tractor-pulled Model 250B Twin, offered by M-R-S (Mississippi Road Services) Manufacturing Co. in 1962 . With a listed 1,400 gross hp and 1,122 fhp available, the unit was capable of handling a 48-cubic yard struck and 58 heaped payload. When the optional sideboards were added, capacity shot up to a very impressive 55-cubic yard struck and 65 heaped payload.

Euclid Road Machinery, later Euclid Division of General Motors, also played an important part in the evolution of the self-propelled scraper. The company is credited with introducing the first twin-engine scraper unit, pulled by an FDT two-axle tractor, in 1949. Full-production models of this type of scraper were introduced in 1950. Then in September 1954, the company unveiled the first production twin-engined scraper pulled by a single-axle, overhung-engined tractor—the revolutionary TS-18. With an engine in the front tractor and a powerplant in the rear scraper unit, it could work in areas that made effective performance impossible for

LeTourneau-Westinghouse Model B Speedpull Triple Fullpak
Among the largest LeTourneau-Westinghouse Model B Speedpull scrapers produced were the special triple units built for Guy F. Atkinson. One of Atkinson's B Speedpulls with Triple B Fullpak scrapers is pictured in Healdsburg, California, in July 1960. The combined capacity for all three scraper units was 69 cubic yards struck and 87 heaped. The triple scraper was 104 feet in length, and weighed in at 156,000 pounds. *ECO Collection*

LeTourneau-Westinghouse Model B Tournapull Tandem Fullpak
After R. G. LeTourneau sold the earth-moving equipment part of his business to Westinghouse Air Brake Company in 1953, the term "Tournapull" became the property of the newly formed LeTourneau-Westinghouse Company. The L-W Model B Tournapull with Tandem B Fullpak scrapers was one of the largest factory-built Tournapull combinations to reach full production when introduced in August 1960. The Model B Tournapull, often referred to as the big "B Pull," was powered by a GM Detroit Diesel 12V-71N engine, rated at 430 gross hp. The capacity rating for the tandem Fullpak scrapers was 46 cubic yards struck and 58 heaped. In 1962, this was increased to 50 cubic yards struck and 60 heaped. The length of the tandem unit was 74 feet, and it had an empty weight of 108,000 pounds. *ECO Collection*

single-engined models. The largest scrapers produced by Euclid were two special-order designs requested by Western Contracting Corporation. The first of these was the two-axle, tractor-pulled TSS-40 model delivered in March 1963. With two engines producing 810 gross hp, and a 40-cubic -yard struck and 52 heaped capacity, the TSS-40 was certainly a very large machine. The second was the massive Tandem TSS-40, also known as the TTSS-40, introduced in August 1964. The TTSS-40 was powered by three Detroit Diesel 16V-71N engines, producing a healthy 1,740 gross hp and 1,690 fhp. The capacity for the tandem scrapers was 80 cubic yards struck and 104 heaped, with a maximum payload of 125 tons. Only five TTSS-40 units were built, and all were for Western Contracting.

Used Euclid scrapers in the field often found themselves being modified into even larger-capacity machines by their owners. By adding another trailer or two, along with a few extra engines thrown in for good measure, contractors could build just the scraper they needed for a particular job. One of the largest of these special units was

the Harris-Euclid Tandem TS-33 "Big Daddy" assembled in 1964. This two-scraper unit was powered by three engines and pulled by a single-axle tractor. The power output was in the neighborhood of 1,500 gross hp. The overall capacity of the two scraper bowls was 66 cubic yards struck and 86 heaped. But as big as this unit was, it paled in comparison to the incredible "Western Tri-Bowl," introduced in May 1966. Fabricated by Western Contracting Corporation, the triple scraper *Tri-Bowl* consisted of a Euclid 43LDT two-axle tractor, and three heavily modified Euclid SS-40 rear scraper units. Power was supplied by four Detroit Diesel 16V-71 engines punching out 2,200 gross hp. The capacity was 120 cubic yards struck and 156 heaped, with a big 188-ton payload rating. Only R. G. LeTourneau built scrapers with larger capacities than the "Tri-Bowl."

Caterpillar Tractor Company entered the self-propelled scraper market in late 1950, with its two-axle tractor DW20 and single-axle tractor DW21. Both of these units were built in prototype form in 1948, but a few years of proving ground testing were

needed to get the production versions right. These early models were both single-engine types. It was not until mid-1962 that Caterpillar would introduce its first two twin-engined scrapers—the Cat 657 and 666 models. Both of these scrapers were big-production earthmovers. The single tractor axle Cat 657 was originally released with power ratings of 980 gross hp and 785 fhp combined. But these figures have steadily increased over the years, with the current 657E model pumping out 995 gross hp and 950 fhp. The capacity has remained consistent at 32 cubic yards struck and 44 heaped. Most in the industry would agree that the 657 series is probably the best all-around large-capacity self-propelled scraper that has ever been built by any manufacturer. In fact, many of the early units from 1962 are still at work today, most of them located in the western United States.

The other big scraper from Caterpillar was the 666 series. With its high-speed, two-axle tractor, the model was capable of carrying 40 cubic yards struck and 54 heaped. In fact, the 666 was the largest-production self-propelled scraper model ever built by Caterpillar, and initial power ratings were the same as the early Cat 657 scraper. The final version, the 666B, was introduced in 1969 with 995 gross hp and 950 fhp, while capacity remained consistent with earlier versions. The 666B was finally discontinued in 1978.

During late 1964, work was in full swing on the San Luis Canal aqueduct project in California. Some of the biggest earth-moving contractors, along with their biggest scraper teams, were working on this mammoth project. One of the largest contractors in the area, Guy F. Atkinson Co., was utilizing R. G. LeTourneau's tandem L-60 and triple L-90 Electric-Diggers on the "Reach One" section of the job. At the same time, Western Contracting Corporation was using its five new Euclid Tandem TSS-40 scrapers on a different location near Modesto, California. Both Caterpillar and Buster Peterson, of Peterson Tractor Co., of San Leandro, California, the local Cat dealer, knew that if they didn't do something quick, a lot of business was going to pass them by. In a crash program, Buster designed a set of tandem 657 scrapers connected together and controlled by a single operator. Special controls were designed to integrate the steering and accelerator systems for multiple-engine use. After the original Tandem 657 unit was tested and refined, an even larger triple-scraper bowl

Euclid Tandem TSS-40
The largest factory-produced scraper built by the General Motors Euclid Division was its Tandem TSS-40, also known as the TTSS-40. The big unit was a special order made for Western Contracting Corporation for use in various construction phases of the San Luis Dam Canal project in California. The TTSS-40 was powered by three Detroit Diesel 16V-71N engines (one in the tractor and one at the end of each scraper unit) for a combined power rating of 1,740 gross hp and 1,690 fhp. The dual scraper had a combined maximum capacity of 86 cubic yards and a 250,000-pound load limit. The empty weight of the unit was 276,000 pounds. The overall length was 108 feet. The first pilot version left the factory in August 1964. A total of five TTSS-40 scrapers were built, all for Western Contracting. *ECO Collection*

Peterson Triple Caterpillar 657

The Triple Caterpillar 657 scraper was the creation of R. A. "Buster" Peterson of Peterson Tractor Co. in California. The scraper consisted of three Cat 657 units connected together to form a single unit controlled by a single operator, located in a cab mounted high over the left rear tire of the front machine. Power was supplied by three Cat D346 eight-cylinder diesel engines and three D343A six-cylinder diesel engines, rated at 2,580 fhp. The capacity of the three high-sided scraper bowls was 150 cubic yards heaped. The overall length was a vast 186 feet. The one-and-only triple 657 was shipped to Peter Kiewit, and it started work around March 1965 on the "Reach Three" section of the San Luis Canal project near Coalinga, California. After 21 months of successful operation, Kiewit purchased an additional Cat 657 from Peterson, and converted the triple unit into two tandem units, each controlled by a single operator. *Peterson* unit was built using the same single-operator, multiple-engine controls.

In March 1965, the Peterson Triple Caterpillar 657 scraper and two Tandem 657 units were shipped to Peter Kiewit & Sons, for use on their part of the "Reach Three" contract, near Coalinga. The giant Triple 657 was an incredible machine. All three scrapers were controlled by a single operator located in an elevated cab, mounted over the left rear wheel of the first unit. From there, the operator kept a sharp eye on the 2580-fhp monster, which was capable of carrying 150 cubic yards of earth. The Tandem 657 units were nothing to

sneeze at either; each was capable of moving 64 cubic yards struck and 88 heaped of dirt. When the three scraper units finished the project 21 months later, more than 22 million cubic yards of earth had been moved by the big Peterson/Cat scrapers. Kiewit then decided to purchase the one-of-a-kind Triple 657, and one additional 657 unit, which was converted into two more sets of single-operator controlled, Tandem 657 scrapers.

Motor Graders

The motor grader is one of those types of earth-moving equipment that is usually

taken for granted. We see them working along roadways, filling and fine grading working areas as only motor graders can. They are the finesse tools of the earth-moving industry. Early versions of graders were nothing more than a wooden board pulled by a horse*—a rather crude but effect means to an end. Later, effective scraping boards were attached to wagons pulled by horses. But the real breakthrough came in 1885, when J. D. Adams introduced the industry's first leaning wheel grader, called the "Little Wonder." With its adjustable leaning wheels, the grader could be used more effectively on sloping sides of roadways. This

Caterpillar 657E

Of all the large-capacity self-propelled scrapers built over the years, the twin-engine Caterpillar 657 series has withstood the test of time since its introduction in 1962; it is today the undisputed leader in its size class. The current Cat 657E, as of 1999, is powered by a Cat 3412E diesel engine in the tractor and a 3408E unit in the rear scraper. The combined power output is 995 gross hp and 950 fhp. The capacity rating is 32 cubic yards struck and 44 heaped. Shown is a 657E Coal Scraper, equipped with the larger, 72.6-cubic yard capacity-scraper bowl for stockpile handling of the lighter weight coal. *Caterpillar*

RayGo Giant

RayGo, Inc., introduced its Giant Earth Leveler grader in late 1969. The big motor grader was actually conceived of by a South Dakota contractor, Ken Harris, in the early 1960s. Harris built large graders out of old Euclid scraper and dozer parts, but it took RayGo to turn the idea into a production reality. The Giant was powered by two Detroit Diesel 8V-71N engines with a combined power rating of 636 gross hp. The machine was articulated in two places so the front power unit could work offset to the rear and eliminate side-draft. The heart of the Giant was its 8,000-pound, 20-foot blade, capable of leveling up to 4,000 cubic yards of earth in an hour. The unit was 46 feet in length, with an operating weight of 105,200 pounds. *ECO Collection*

Caterpillar 666

The largest scraper ever produced by Caterpillar was its 666 model. Introduced in 1962, this high-speed unit enjoyed a solid reputation as a big-production earthmover. The 666 was powered by two engines, an eight-cylinder Cat D346 diesel in the tractor and a six-cylinder Cat D343A in the rear scraper unit, rated at 980 gross hp and 785 fhp combined. Later variations would see power increases up to 900 fhp. The capacity for the scraper bowl was 40 cubic yards struck and 54 heaped. The length of the big scraper was 56 feet, 8 inches. Empty weight of the unit was 136,000 pounds. In the series, the last version of the scraper, the 666B, was the most powerful, carrying a power output of 950 fhp. The 666B was in production from 1969 to 1978. *ECO*

Champion 80T
The second-largest motor grader ever built was the Champion 100T. Originally built by the Dominion Road Machinery Company in Ontario, Canada, the massive leveler was unveiled as the 80T in the fall of 1975 at a Toronto equipment trade exposition. In 1977, the company's product identification of Champion replaced the Dominion name in the firm's title. Champion officially introduced the 100T grader at the October 1978 American Mining Congress show in Las Vegas, Nevada, where it picked up the nickname of "Big Mudder." All of the 80T/100T graders' superstructures were fabricated by a specialized welding subcontractor in Minneapolis, Minnesota, with the final assembly taking place at facilities operated by Champion in South Carolina. Shown at the Cyprus Bagdad Copper Mine in June 1978, one of the early 80T units is tested under the hot Arizona sun. *ECO Collection*

leaning wheel feature can be found in all of today's modern machines.

In 1919, the Russell Grader Manufacturing Company built the first self-propelled grader. This prototype unit consisted of a two-wheel Allis-Chalmers tractor front, with a grader attached to the rear. The first true motor grader in production was the Caterpillar Auto Patrol, introduced in 1931. The Auto Patrol's rear drivetrain and front grader assembly were built as a single unit, not as an option to a conventional tractor. Though the original Caterpillar No. 9 Auto Patrol utilized only a single rear-drive axle at first, in 1934 later models, No. 10 and No. 11, were offered with tandem-drive rear axles, which has become a key feature of the modern motor grader.

As motor graders began finding large construction and mining applications, their size increased dramatically. In 1963, Caterpillar introduced one of its most popular big graders, the No. 16. Powered by a 225-fhp Cat Diesel, the No. 16 was considered quite powerful for its day. It was also equipped with a fairly large moldboard

blade, measuring 14 feet across. But soon after the initial release of the No. 16, the moldboard width was increased to 16 feet. Other model introductions were the 250-fhp Cat 16G in 1973 and the 275-fhp Cat 16H in late 1994.

In 1969, RayGo, Inc., of Minneapolis, Minnesota, created much excitement in the earth-moving industry with the introduction of its Giant Earth Leveler. The concept for the Giant dated back to the early 1960s, when Ken Harris, a contractor and Euclid dealership owner in South Dakota, built a few experimental motor graders referred to as "Harris Blades." These graders were built primarily out of used Euclid scraper and TC-12 dozer bits and pieces. RayGo refined Harris' concept into a full-production model—with mixed results. The Giant was powered by two diesel engines, generating 636 gross hp combined. The massive moldboard was 20 feet wide and weighed four tons. An optional 24-foot blade was also available for special working conditions. But the mining industry as a whole was wary of new-concept

machines and really never gave the Giant a fighting chance.

In the same year the RayGo Giant was introduced, CMI Corporation of Oklahoma released its rather large Autoblade hydrostatic-drive motor grader. Like the big RayGo, the Autoblade was double-articulated and was powered by two separate, two-axle engine modules, totaling 450 gross hp. The centrally located cab mounting could be swiveled to face the Autoblade's changing direction of travel, and the blade width was 18 feet. However, this design found no more industry acceptance than the RayGo Giant, and the Autoblade was soon abandoned.

The next company to try market a large motor grader was the Dominion Road Machinery Company, located in Ontario, Canada, and better known as Champion. The Dominion name dates back to 1910, but the company's early roots in road-building equipment extend back as far as 1875.

In the fall of 1975, Dominion introduced its massive motor grader—the Champion 80T. Over the next few years, prototype models were put through a vigorous field testing program. While this was going on, the name of the company officially changed in 1977 to Champion Road Machinery. In October 1978, at the American Mining Congress show in Las Vegas, Nevada, the giant motor grader was officially introduced as the Champion 100T "Big Mudder." The 100T was definitely a big grader. It carried a 24-foot-wide moldboard blade, with its power rated at 700 gross hp. Its 101-ton working weight made it over 48 tons heavier than the RayGo Giant. The tandem-drive 100T looked like a conventional motor grader on steroids, but the market for a machine this size was severely limited. After numerous attempts at expanding that market, Champion threw in the towel in 1989 and sold the 100T product line to Dom-Ex, Inc., of Hibbing, Minnesota. Dom-Ex marketed the grader as the Dom-Ex 100T, and put a few trial upgraded Champion units into various mining sites, but to no avail. To date, Dom-Ex has never built a 100T of its own. In early 1997, Champion Road Machinery became a wholly owned subsidiary of AB Volvo of Sweden.

Shortly after the introduction of the Champion 100T, O&K Orenstein & Koppel of Germany tried its hand at building a big grader. In late 1979, O&K introduced the G350 grader. Though not as large as the massive Champion, the O&K was by no means a small machine. Power was supplied by a 360-gross-hp diesel engine, and it was originally equipped with a 16-foot-wide moldboard, though later versions would get a much larger 19-foot blade. But as with many other pieces of earth-moving equipment introduced in the early 1980s, bad economic conditions put the G350 model line into a tailspin. The last year O&K offered the G350 was 1991. In all, only 34 units were ever built.

Many manufacturers tried and failed to market a large motor grader over the years. But it took Caterpillar, the company that created the revolutionary Auto Patrol, to build and market a true, full-production machine—the Cat 24H. The 24H grader actually started development in 1987 as the 18H. But as the project developed, the basic design increased in size. Prototype testing started in 1995, with the first preproduction field machine shipped in late 1995 to the AMAX Eagle Butte Coal Mine, just north of Gillette, Wyoming, in the Powder River Basin. Powered by a single Cat diesel engine, the 24H pumps out a healthy 540 gross hp and 500 fhp. The moldboard on the grader measures 24 feet across. At its 68-ton working weight, the Caterpillar 24H is larger than the RayGo Giant, but smaller than the Champion 100T. The 24H grader was designed for large-scale mining operations, and was primarily intended to maintain haul roads, including the loading and dumping sites. It has

Champion 100T
The Champion 100T was powered by a single Detroit Diesel 16V-71T engine, rated at 700 gross hp, with a Cummins unit as an option. The large blade was 24 feet wide and 56 inches high. The length of the entire machine was 50 feet, 3 inches, with an 18-foot height to the top of the cab. Operating weight of the 100T was 202,000 pounds. In 1989, Champion sold the rights to the 100T to Dom-Ex Inc. of Hibbing, Minnesota. Today, it is marketed as the Dom-Ex 100T, though none have been built since the sale, due to lack of demand. This Champion 100T is pictured in July 1991 at Syncrude's oil sand mining operation in northern Alberta. *Keith Haddock*

Caterpillar 24H

The Caterpillar 24H is the largest motor grader currently produced, as of 1999, by the company. The big grader is powered by a 12-cylinder Cat 3412E diesel engine, rated at 540 gross hp and 500 fhp. The moldboard blade is 24 feet wide and 42 inches high. The length of the grader is 51 feet, 10 inches, with a maximum overall working weight of 136,611 pounds. The Cat 24H was originally identified as the 18H early in its design phase. The first preproduction prototype unit started testing in 1995, with customer deliveries commencing in 1996. *ECO* found great acceptance in the mining industry, and as of 1999 it is the largest motor grader currently in full production.

A history of the largest motor graders wouldn't be complete without mentioning the truly massive ACCO Grader. It was built in the early 1980s by contractor Umberto Acco of Portogruaro, near Venice, in northern Italy. The ACCO Grader is simply the largest motor grader ever built. Even the Champion 100T looks like a toy when compared to this behemoth. Despite its enormous size, however, the ACCO Grader has not been particularly successful. In fact, only two units were built, an experimental prototype and a second, more refined, machine. The ACCO Grader is powered by two Caterpillar diesel engines—one 1,000-gross-hp, 12-cylinder engine in the rear, driving two axles, and one 700-gross-hp unit in the front, driving a single axle. At about 200 tons, the giant ACCO requires six double-tire wheel assemblies, totaling 12 tires, to offset the grader's huge weight. But the grader was never sold. The American embargo against Libya in the 1980s caused the cancellation of both the ACCO Grader and its partner ACCO Dozer. The grader has worked a few jobs here and there, but for the most part it spends its time parked outside ACCO's main facilities in Italy; the original prototype is stored indoors, away from sight.

ACCO Giant Grader

The largest motor graders ever produced were the massive experimental ACCO Graders from the early 1980s. Conceived of by Umberto Acco and fabricated at his facilities in Italy, the giant 12-tire grader looks like no other. It is powered by two Caterpillar diesel engines—one 8-cylinder, 700-gross-hp unit in the front, and one 12-cylinder, 1,000-gross-hp powerplant in the rear, totaling 1,700 gross hp. The moldboard is a staggering 33 feet across, with the option of additional 5-foot wing blade extensions.

The grader is 69 feet in length, and weighs in at approximately 200 tons. Only two experimental ACCO Graders were ever built, and the second unit has only worked five or so jobs for the city of Bibione, reconditioning the sandy beaches on the Adriatic Coast. The first prototype unit is in storage. The second grader is pictured here in October 1997, at Acco's main equipment yard in Italy. *Klaus Mayr*

INDEX